OM NAMASHIVAYA
Thiruvasagham

OM NAMASHIVAYA
Thiruvasagham
(Explanatory Notes)

(Recited by Saint Manickavasaghar—9th Century)

Translated into English by
Swamiji IRAIANBAN

abhinav publications

First published in India 1999

© Swamiji Iraianban

Publishers

Shakti Malik
Abhinav Publications
E-37, Hauz Khas
New Delhi-110016 (INDIA)
Phones: 6566387, 6562784, 6524658
Fax: 91-11-6857009
e-mail: shakti@nde.vsnl.net.in
         abhinav.abhinaf@axcess.net.in

ISBN 81-7017-373-6

Phototypeset in Garamond 12pt by

Tara Chand Sons
Naraina, New Delhi-110028

Printed at

D.K. Fine Art Press Pvt. Ltd.
Ashok Vihar, Delhi

Contents

Preface

"Thiruvasagham" is the most sacred literature in Tamil which glorifies the manifestations of Lord Shiva. It is kept as the first reference book in Lord Shiva's library itself. The "Gita" is told by the Lord to man (Sri Krishna to Arjuna). The Thirukkural is recited by a man to Mankind (Thiruvalluvar) and "Thiruvasagham" is recited by a man (Saint Manickavasaghar) which is heard and pleased by Lord Shiva Himself.

"Thiruvasagham" is a treasure of priceless value. It is a devotional hymn which occupies the highest place in the hymnology of the literature of Saivites. It is a masterpiece and is second to none in the whole range of Tamil literature. "Thiruvasagham" is the only work which, according to tradition, had been written by the Lord Himself. It is the Gita of the Saivite world. It is an immortal classic which melts the hearts of its readers and mellows even a stone.

We have become eternally wedded to this sacred "Thiruvasagham" either due to our parentage or due to our past Karmas. Our humble self has soulfully dedicated itself to this spiritual storehouse of Tamil. It has been further consecrated by our having committed to memory all the 51 chapters. Our overwhelming devotion to saint Manickavasaghar first of all blossomed into a Tamil anthology called "Manickavasaghar Maalai" or "A garland of praise of Manickavasaghar"—a hundred Tamil verses praising the saint and commenting on his teachings. It is needless to point out here that this new and interesting English version of Thiruvasagham took our soul by storm and pinned us to the pleasant task of reading it, from wrapper to wrapper.

Tamil literature is extremely rich in devotional poetry which has no parallel in the literature of any other language. Unfortunately, those who have no knowledge of the Tamil language and even many whose mother tongue happens to be Tamil are not today fully aware of the beauty and greatness of this class of Tamil literature. The name of the Saivite Saint Manickavasaghar is one of the greatest in the history of the Tamil devotional literature. "Thiruvasagham" is his greatest musical composition.

It is the peculiar glory of Tamil literature that its great treasures are enshrined in devotional songs. These devotional songs emanated from such illustrious saints and sages as Manickavasaghar, other Nayanmars and Azhwars, besides eminent poets and philosophers like Sri Sankarar, Ramanujar, Thiruvalluvar, Sekkizhar and Kambar who were all immersed in religious knowledge and fervour. The value of the songs cannot be overrated. For they are the outcome of intense devotion of a great saint to whom God manifested Himself in visible form. Great scholars dedicated themselves to the task of translating the songs of Thiruvasagham, but found a number of passages beyond their capacity. In 1900, Dr. G.U. Pope, a Christian missionary, translated "Thiruvasagham" in English. It is the first and indubitably an excellent and scholarly piece of work. It is odd but true that many Indians including persons whose mother tongue is Tamil could realize the greatness of Manickavasaghar's Thiruvasagham only after reading Dr. G.U. Pope's translation in English. This reverent Christian has been included by us among the canonized saints of Saivites. We think of him with love and gratitude, are proofs that he is deemed by us not only as a doctorate of divinity but also as one who has divinity of a doctorate.

English occupies a unique position among the languages of the world. It is spoken and understood by the largest number of people in the world. So any literary production which seeks to make a universal appeal should be translated into English. It is the most gratifying to know that there is already a German translation of Holy Thiruvasagham. Even French scholars are said to be eager to take advantage of the English translation of this great work. It is our sincere wish and earnest prayer that this book will soon be translated in other languages also, so that the message of Saint Manickavasaghar will reach every corner of the world.

The essence of Thiruvasagham (656 verses) can be realized chapter-wise:

1. Shivapuranam has a sub-title called "Shiva's Ways of Old". This chapter refers to the way in which God supervises the evolution of the soul through different transformations from one state to another towards the state of a Jeevanmuktha and Mukthi (Eternal Saturation).

2. This chapter—Keerthi Thiru Ahaval or "Sacred Song of Shiva's Renowned Acts"—deals with the historic and time-bound acts of Shiva who appears on earth in varied forms of succour. He celebrates His sincere devotees in the towns and cities of Tamilnadu. Chidambaram is considered to be the heart-centre of the world. And Shiva's mystic dance at Chidambaram is said to be symbolic of His dance within the hearts of His Creatures.

3. Thiru Andappakudhi or the Evolution and Cycle of the Universe has an introduction of 28 lines. After this the praises of Lord Shiva are intermingled with somewhat puzzling but skilful allegories. He is addressed with a mixture of awe and simple affection which has a peculiar effect. This personal relation of God as manifested Guru to His disciples and devotees is the most prominent through all Manickavasaghar's poems.

4. Potri Thiru Ahaval is the hymn in the Ahavalpa
    metre in which nearly 135 lines out of 225 end in
    the word "Potri" or "Praise". "The origin of the
    Universe" which is the sub-title refers to the soul
    obtaining the rarest human birth, its survival of the
    embryonic life and its many dangers in the mother's
    womb. "The pilgrim's progress" can be a more
    appropriate title given to this chapter. This, in fact,
    is a hymn of praise, a hallelujah in the full sense of
    the word.

5. Thiruchatthakam—Chatthakam means a composi-
    tion of one hundred stanzas. The last word of each
    stanza is repeated at the start of each following
    stanza. Its essence is "Wondrous spiritual steadfast-
    ness". This chapter describes the ten-fold method
    of granting grace to our saint by Lord Shiva. The
    course of his thoughts and the character of his
    mental struggles between rapturous and realizing
    devotion and cold hard-heartedness can be felt.
    This may seem to lead him temporarily to give
    himself up to lustful pleasures.

6. Neethal Vinnappam—the sub-title of which is "For-
    sake me not". This hymn is considered as one of
    the sage's most interesting compositions. In the
    midst of a terrible struggle a genuine human cry
    for divinehelp is seen throughout. It is full of the
    strongest emotions.

7. Thiruvembavai—'the mystic songs of the maid-
    ens'—is a morning hymn. It is said to have been
    composed for the use of women at Arunachalam
    (Thiruvannamalai). For it was a custom among
    women to celebrate with great activities of joy a
    festival in honour of God Shiva and Goddess Sakthi.
    During that time, the women of the city, of all ages,
    got up before dawn, for ten successive days. They
    went about the neighbourhood arousing their com-
    panions from house to house and proceeded to

bathe in the sacred tank.

8. Thiruammanai is again said to be composed at the sacred shrine of Annamalai. "Ammanai" is one of the 64 kinds of Tamil prabhandas. It is a play of balls in which three maidens usually partake. The subject of their songs is God or the time of a hero. They sing while each one of them is casting the ball up and catching it and passing it on to the other. The first maiden sings in the form of a query, the 2nd maid answers the query in song and the 3rd sings the reason thereof. In this poem, one maid is the singer cum player. The last line of every stanza in this poem is "Let's sing the rapture great", hence the sub-title of this piece is given as "Rapturous joy". In this poem, the saint recounts his own experience in some verses while he puts words into the mouth of the playing maids, in other verses.

9. Thirupporchunnam or the "Sacred Golden Dust". The sage saw maidens pounding gold dust in Thillai. As they were pounding, they were heard to be singing meaningless songs; so he composed these 20 verses, in a somewhat loose metre, to be sung in rhythm with the pestles.

10. Thirukkothumbi or the "Bumble-Bee" is addressed to the humming bees or winged beetles, it is probably the dragon fly; here the Soul is addressed and urged to seek Lord Shiva's Feet. The inner meaning of this poem is identity with Shiva. For, the bee of one's own mind is addressed to go to the Lord and blow. It seems the bee is a favourite creature of poets of all nations.

11. Thirutthellenam is a kind of maidens' game where a number of maidens beat their palms to the tune of songs sung in chorus by them all. They stand in circle or in position of opposite rows. This again is a case of mundane instrument of innocent de-

light in the hands of the maidens. It is being magnified and sublimated by our saint into a medium of soul-culture and mighty bliss.

12. Thiruchazhal is also another kind of maidens' play. This must be very much like the modern play among young girls, where one poses a question in rhyme and another answers in rhyme. The song of sazhalo, though sung by two persons alone and made up of two lines of questions and latter two lines of answers, is similar to our modern quiz but not in rhymed words of poetry. Its meaning here has been stated to be the sport of Arulsakthi or the merciful grace of Lord Shiva. It is only on account of Lord Shiva's boundless compassion for the human beings that He condescends to assume a visible form and adorn it with white ashes, black cobras, the Ganges and the Moon. This song was the consequence of the story connected with the incident of the Buddhist king of Ceylon challenging the Saiva leaders in a theological controversy, and being defeated, and thereby describing the Supremacy of Lord Shiva through the mouth of the dumb girl who was restored speech by Saint Manickavasaghar.

13. Thiruppoovalli or the "Play of plucking lilies". It is a play of a number of young maidens joining together to pluck flowers as well as lilies from the water tanks. The inner meaning is getting rid of Maya matter. Maya's voluptuous and ravishing beauty is symbolised by the colour, beauty and smell and softness of the flowers. Hence, plucking away these flowers really means the act of removing the enslaving charm of Maya.

14. Thiruwunthiyar—"Wunthu" is also a play concerning young girls. The word Unthi is used for the shuttle-cock or ball which the players cause to "Fly

Soft". Our saint has found this brick of a game in the hands of maidens and converted it into gold by his sublimating and divine words.

15. Thirutthonokkam literally means "aiming at the shoulders" for it ends up with placing the hands of each opposite pair on the other. The inner meaning of this chapter is said to be "Prapancha Suddhi". In some lines, this is said to be symbolic of the approach of the soul to Lord Shiva's Feet. It means the soul should not be cheated by the false appearance of the world but should, after enough discrimination, surrender itself to Lord Shiva and thus convert all its acts into penance.

16. Thirupponoosal or "Moving the Golden Swing" is the last of the series of pastimes of womenfolk in this work, though it is not a game properly so called. The inner meaning of this poem is said to be "Arul Suddhi" which means the purification of the soul attained as a result of its blending with Grace.

17. Annaippatthu or the "Ten stanzas of Motherhood" is a series of exclamations uttered by a little girl to her mother. We wish to point out that the whole poem is supposed to be sung by the mother of a maid used to convey these ideas and words to the former. Attaining the plenitude of the soul in union with Shiva is the inner meaning of this poem. This Athmapuram is attained when the soul filled with the Lord loses its self-consciousness and becomes frenzied and lost in Him.

18. Kuyilppatthu or the "Ten verses of the Kuyil". The kuyil is often referred to in these poems. In this poem, he calls upon the kuyil to join him in the praises of his master. Mystically, the kuyil is the human soul. The lady-love experiences the pangs of separation from her Lord. This separation is painfully delayed. So, she appeals to the kuyil to

go to her Lord and carry her message to Him and call Him to come. She describes to the kuyil the nature and qualities of her Lord.

19. Thirutthasangam or the "Sacred Ten Insignia". It is entitled as Tasangam as it mentions the ten Royal Insignia pertaining to Lord Shiva. Each stanza (Venba—4 lines) is divided into 2 halves—the 1st part being the question and the latter part is its answer. The 1st part is obviously the question put by the lady-love to the parrot. The 2nd part or the answer may be taken either as the answer taught to the parrot by the maid herself or the answer is supposed to be given by the parrot to the maid's question. We prefer the latter view.

20. Thiruppalliezhuchi or "Song of rousing from the sacred couch". In truth, after the long night's restful sleep, the soul revived in energy wakes up to start its fresh day's work and duties. All ceremonials what we call service to God in the temples is only euphemism. In reality, it is what we do unto ourselves. Feeding God means feeding living beings. So also the waking up God means and includes awakening our own selves only. We only sing about a thing we have already done. We have awakened ourselves.

21. Kovil Moothathiruppathigham or the "Ancient Temple Hymn". Actually, in eight out of ten stanzas a reference to Ponnambalam is found! "Anadi Satharyam" is said to be the meaning to this poem. But the old puranam says that this chapter indicates the gain of grace in Chidambaram and that is correct.

22. Kovil Thiruppathigham or the "Sacred Temple Lyric"—the old puranam speaks of this chapter as a yearning of the soul for the Lord at Perunthurai. Hence, though it was composed at Thillai, its appeal is to Lord Shiva of Thirupperunthurai.

23. Chethilappatthu or the "Ten verses of Despondency". This poem bewails the interference of egoism in the complete enjoyment of bliss by the soul. The old puranam says that quietful self is not yet dead—which means my egoism is not yet eliminated.

24. Adaikkalappatthu or the "Ten verses of Refuge". The old puranam says that these ten verses of refuge were sung to prevent strong "deeds" from gripping the soul.

25. Aasaippatthu or the "Ten verses of Desire". It expresses the desire of the soul for grace, in order to detach itself from the world and the body and to attach itself to His blissful grace. Hence, it is called the decad of desire. "Athma Lakshanam" is the sub-title of this poem which means knowing the Athmaroopam.

26. Athisayappatthu or the "Ten verses of Wonder"— the sub-heading of this chapter given by an old note is "Mukthi Illakkanam" (Grammar of Ecstasy) or "Song of Moksha". The ancient puranam says it means the expression of exultation and wonder at the phenomenon of the Lord's kingdom in having removed the soul from the world of bondage and `maya' and placed it in the unchanging and ennobling company of his Holy saints.

27. Punarchippatthu or the "Ten verses of Mystic Nuptial". The significance of this poem as some notes give is "Advaita Lakshanam". It is the uniting of God and the soul in a manner which could be described as neither one nor two. The old puranam explains this poem as expressing the anxiety of the soul to get mystically locked up in the embrace of God who is at once love and bliss. This poem belongs to the variety of mystic wedlock of a very elevated character.

28. Vazhappatthu or the "Ten verses of disgust with

Life". This poem is an appeal to God Shiva to call the soul unto Himself as there is no other help for it in this wide world. It is also because it cannot bear life here on this earth. Some notes are of the opinion that it indicates "Mukthi Upayam" or the way to achieve Liberation.

29. Arulppatthu or the "Ten verses of Divine Grace" —the subject is purification of the soul from Mahamaya. Mahamaya suddhi means freedom from delusions. It means giving up worldly attachments in disgust and thirsting for the Lord's Feet. The old puranam says that this chapter appeals to God to come and ask the soul "Why call'st me" when the soul yearns to leave this world and reach His Feet.

30. Thirukkazhukkundrappathigham or the "Hymn of Sacred Eagle Mount". The original name of the Hill, Vedagiri, has become practically superseded by the modern name Kazhukkundram. Saint Manickava-saghar had a divine perception of Lord Shiva at Perunthurai and it disappeared the moment the Lord had finished His mission on earth namely the conoisation of Manickavasaghar.

31. Kandappatthu or the "Ten verses of Darshan". This chapter deals with Nittha darshan of Lord Shiva. This means that he has seen the Rapture-bliss of Lord Shiva. It lifts his soul up from the mire of the deceitful senses and the maya bound worldly life and makes him its own, within the Holy Thillai.

32. Prarthanaippatthu or the "Ten verses of Petitioning". This poem heartily appeals to Lord Shiva to plunge the soul in endless bliss and not to leave her at all.

33. Kuzhaitthappatthu or the "Ten verses of Self-Surrender". The inner meaning is "Athma Nivedhanam". It is an offering of the soul to God as an oblation. The soul gives up her self-agency and surrenders

her self-will and abides in God. This is the climax of Holy Thiruvasagham. She begins to live, move and have her being in God.

34. Wuyirunnippatthu or the "Ten verses of devoured soul". It means that the soul which has the good fortune of enjoying the bliss gets lost in the flood of rapture. The soul loses its natural characteristics of its embodied state and becomes identical with the Bliss of Lord Shiva.

35. Achchappatthu or the "Ten verses of Fear". The soul which is submerged and soaked in the flood of Sivananda or the Supreme Ecstasy in Advaitic union, will fear and dread everything or every person alien to such a bliss. This is what is meant by absorption in Aanandha.

36. Thiruppandippathigham or the "Sacred Pandi Hymn"—the inner significance of this poem is profuse growth of bliss. It is an appeal to the world to come and enjoy the same bliss which our saint has enjoyed at the hands of the warrior King of Pandiland, i.e., Lord Shiva who comes riding a horse.

37. Piditthappatthu or the "Ten verses of devout grip". The inner meaning is `holding the Lord in one's firm and tenacious grasp with a sense of security and assurance that He will not give one the slip. This poem is said to explain to other souls the rapture and joy of Mukthi or union with Lord Shiva.

38. Thiruvesaravu or the "Sacred Grief". This is explained as the soul's complete renunciation of its own agency or will and becoming merged in God. Thus it assumes or attunes itself, its thoughts and deeds to the sacred will of Lord Shiva.

39. Thiruppulambal or "The sacred Lament". It means letting forth our lamentation to the Lord and appealing to Him to grant us the grace with which we could cry and weep for Him as a calf does for its mother, cow.

40. Kulappatthu or the "Ten verses of divine Thillai". This means sending forth the thanks of the soul to Lord Shiva for His bounteous grace for having given the soul the privilege of enjoying His ravishing bliss without interruption and in a uniform measure. Hence, it is called uninterrupted Divine Experience.

41. Arbhuthappatthu or the "Ten verses of Miracle". It is a loud cry of satisfaction and praise by a soul who was wallowing deep in the mire of worldly lusts. For he has suddenly been given to taste the ambrosial divine grace and has been given altogether the perfect release.

42. Sennippatthu or the "Ten verses of the Head". The inner meaning is "The fruitioning of bliss of Lord Shiva". This chapter describes the beauty of how the Feet of the soul's Guru—Lord Shiva shine upon her crown, so it is called the "decade of Head".

43. Thiruvaarthai or the "Sacred Word"—"Vaarthai", the word is the instrument, instructing about Brahman or God. This chapter has received that name since it speaks about God teaching the saint about God. The sub-heading means "Know when taught about that which You Yourself cannot know".

44. Ennappathigham or "Devout Musings". This chapter is so called because it gives expression to the thoughts and musings of the soul that it wants to be rid of birth on earth, to be full of God's love, to have the sight of God's form etc.

45. Yaatthiraippatthu or the "Ten verses of Pilgrimage". This would mercifully invite all fellow-beings to accompany the saint towards the goal of Shiva's Feet, since the time has arrived when he could leave this maya world and lead to his master's Feet. The inner meaning is said to be "Experience of expressing the divine ex perience transcending our capacity".

46. Thiruppadaiezhuchi or the "Spiritual mobilization"—the sub-title 'Prapancha Por' means elimination of the seeds of malam or bonds. This is an invitation or bugle call to the devotees to lift up their arms in crusade against the forces of Mahamaya.

47. Thiruvenba or the "Sacred Stanza"—the sub-heading of the chapter is "The state of those who have attained". It deals with the act of grace which converts all that it touches into Lord Shiva.

48. Pandaya Naanmarai—"The Reality of divine grace"—is the sub-heading of this chapter. This poem asserts that only those saints who worship Perunthurai and its Lord will be saved from births and bonds.

49. Thiruppadaiaatchi or the "The Spiritual Exploits of the sacred Hordes". The sub-heading "the elimination of soul's egoistic experience" would mean that the moment the Lord enters the soul all the lumber of egoism would exit from the soul.

50. Aanandamaalai or the "Garland of Rapture"—desire for enjoyment of bliss of Lord Shiva, is the sub-heading of this poem. It means the obliteration of Kriya sakthi in the midst of the enjoyment of excessive bliss of Lord Shiva.

51. Achchoppathigham or the "Hymn of Highest Bliss"—"Incapacity to gauge the Attained Supreme Bliss"—is the sub-title of the poem, which means being at a loss to standardize the measure and rareness of the supreme bliss that one has attained.

The explanatory notes and comments to Thiruvasagham appended to the text, it is hoped, will be of some use in widening the intellectual and spiritual horizon of the people of the East and the West. There are some who lay separatist claims to spiritual monopoly to the exclusion of the others. We would feel gratified and grateful if, even in a small measure, these notes and comments instil and confirm in the minds of the readers the Eternal Truth that the East and the West meet together and shake hands on the spiritual Everest of the Himalayan Faith.

Such a work as "Thiruvasagham" is and must be the property of humanity at large, though Divine Providence had designed its origin in Tamilnadu. This is not only a book of all time but "one for all clime". So, in such a way, we must also go to the deepest depth of the spiritual harmony of Thiruvasagham and thus we may make our birth a useful one. By God's Grace, we are giving notes to the Holy Thiruvasagham and hope this will help all the aspirants to taste the inner nectar of the most sacred spiritualism in this mundane world and thereby, we can be merged with full-fledged peace and Shanthi.

Thiruchittrambalam.

Om Shivarppanam.

Swamiji Iraianban

Life-Sketch of Saint Manickavasaghar

Thiruvadhavoorar was the name of a child who was born to a Brahmin couple (Sambupadhasiruthayar Sivagnanavathy), in the village of Thiruvadhavoor. This village is situated in Madurai. The child's father belonged to a sect of Brahmins called Ammathiya. It was from this sect of Ammathiya Brahmins that ministers of state and mighty administrators were appointed. Thiruvadhavoorar proved that he had unusual and remarkable abilities to learn. He was a wonderful example of learning. Before he reached his 16th year, he had mastered all branches of knowledge, both sacred as well as secular. He then presented a pleasing picture of perfect beauty and finished culture. He was an enviable young descendant of an ancient and renowned family. His physical attractiveness was matched by his mental achievements. This boy-bachelor in many respects was an Indian hope of an English Wolsey.

The fame of this rarest gem of a young Brahmin reached the Pandya King who was ruling then. His name is given as Arimarthanan by the author of Thiruvilayadal puranam, Paranjyothi Munivar. But, history does not approve of this name. Anyway, the learned Thiruvadhavoorar was invited to the court by the King. He was so much attracted by the person and talents of young Vadhavoorar that he immediately appointed him as his Prime Minister. He also gave the title of

"Thennavan Brahmarayar" to the young scholar. The King also gave him extraordinary and unlimited powers over the kingdom and its administration. The young Prime Minister managed the administration of the kingdom in such a manner as if he was born for it. Prosperity flourished and justice was ruling the land. Yet it cannot be said that the Prime Minister gave his heart and soul to the job. Yet in spite of himself he felt a strange feeling of separation between himself and the unlimited powers he employed over his vast kingdom. There was a wide gap which seemed to separate the soul from his minister's work as a whole. It was all a case of Wolsey in the opposite direction. While all along the English Prime Minister was too trying to associate himself with power and increasing his own position and rank, our Brahmarayar was psychologically detaching himself from the power and glory of the state. He attached himself more and more to spiritual life. He was restless and all too eager to seek spiritual Guru. He wanted a Guru to lead him to salvation in this birth itself. His spiritual thirst increased with every day. Time was heavily hanging on him because a day that did not take him to a guru was considered a day that was wasted. But soon there came an end to the mental agony of the Prime Minister.

One day, some messengers informed the King that equestrian wing of the standing army was weak and exhausted. They said that that was the right moment to fill up the cavalry forces because ships loaded with war-horses had just then arrived at the harbour of the Chola country. Here, we are of the opinion that the horses must have come from Arabia only. Since, during the time of Vadhavoorar, there was well-established cultural and commercial trade between the west and India, particularly the Pandyan country. The King called the Prime Minister himself and asked him to go to the port that was mentioned and personally transact the purchase of enough number of horses accordingly the minister was also given an enormous treasure for that purpose.

The Prime Minister as the head of a vast army started on his mission. After passing through hills and dales the ministerial party was nearing a place called "Thirupperunthurai". At this place, he heard a chorus of divine songs, as if sung by a thousand strains. It was too attractive to let the party pass away without enquiring into the cause of the source from where the divine chorus was heard. The Prime Minister had now arrived at the proper psychological moment which was a turning point in his life. He got down from his palanquin. He became unconscious of everything else and slowly made his way to the spot from where the sound was coming. As soon as he reached the spot, the sight that he saw was too delightful and too joyous that it cannot be expressed in words. He saw a mystic Guru who had a rosary of scarlet Eleocarpus beads around his head, throat and breast. He was smeared with sacred ashes of dazzling white. He had a third eye of fire in the centre of his shining forehead, and a sacred book in his hand. He was surrounded by 999 sivanadiars (devotees of Lord Shiva).

Our Vadhavoorar knew that the book in his hand was the Holy "Sivagnanabotham", which would enlighten the soul about the soul and God. Immediately, he dropped off all his official dress—the dress of a Prime Minister and became dead unto this world. The hair on his body stood up on its edges, tears flowed down his cheeks and he fell stretched out on the ground at the feet of the Saviour. Then the Guru initiated him into the mystic manthra. He introduced him to the doctrines of Saiva Siddandha philosophy by planting of the sacrament. The minister had now become the beggar. He became charged with spiritual fervour and God-intoxication. Gems of words wove themselves into magnificent garlands and rained forth from his silver tongue. The Guru was delighted with the musical verses, of the convert's soulful words, which have no equal. He christened him as "Manickavasaghar"—HE, of Ruby words—and blessed Him. Now, Vadhavoorar had become so completely transformed that he became the Guru's own word and action. He spent away all the funds in his possession in feeding thousands of Shiva's followers and in building and repairing the Temple at Thirupperunthurai.

Days passed by and the Pandya King came to know about this fact, issued an order to his ex-minister to immediately return with all the horses. Manickavasaghar did not know what to do, except to take refuge at the Feet of His Guru. The Guru came to his rescue and commanded him to go at once to Madurai and inform the King that the fleet of horses would reach there on the Avani Moolam day (according to the Tamil calendar, the month, day and the star is represented). He also handed over a bright ruby to the saint to be presented to the King in person.

The King, when he was presented with the rare ruby by his ex-minister, became mightily pleased and complimented Manickavasaghar. He also assured him about the definite arrival of the horses on Avani Moolam day. But the King learnt from the spies of the court that though Avanimoolam was very near, there was no trace of the sound of the horses' hoofs anywhere near Madurai. The King became very doubtful and ordered for the saint to be punished and put in prison. He was wailing and appealing to his master to come to his help. And the master came to the disciple's rescue on the day when Avanimoolam came. Just at the appointed hour, the King saw the whole of Madurai city filled with horses ridden on and led by strange looking foreigners. The King became pleased once again and ordered the release of the Saint Manickavasaghar. The Lord had come there in the disguise of the Arabic horse-seller. He displayed the whole cavalry of horses to the King and handed over their charge to him. The King felt that he had made a much better bargain than his money's worth. As was the King's custom, he presented clothes and gold to the merchant prince. But as was the custom with the horse-seller of Arabia, he simply took the presents at the end of his cane and threw them on the horses without bowing to the King and thanking him. The King became angry but was calmed down by the saint who gave him a satisfactory explanation.

The merchant departed that day, but at the middle of that night a strange thing happened. The whole of Madurai city was thrown into fear. The newly arrived horses had changed themselves into jackals. They all ran out here and there, with great speed and in a disorderly manner. They ran out of the stables with their ugly howlings. While they were running away, they brought damage by biting other horses and whomsoever they met on the way. This distressing story reached the Pandya King. The King became angry once again and directed all his anger on the poor saint. Manickavasaghar once again became a victim of torture and punishment at the hands of the King's servants. This time he was actually fried, as it were, on the hot sand beds of the river Vaigai.

Once again the saint sent forth his wailing appeal to his master for help. And the master without fail rushed to his rescue by making refreshes to appear in the Vaigai river. There was a flood. The flood threatening the safety of the Madurai city itself. The King ordered that each family should be allotted a portion of the river-bank to be repaired and safeguarded. One, Vanthi, an old and helpless woman, who was pudding vendor was also given her allotted share of work, in repairing and safeguarding the river-bank. She did not know what to do, for she had no male companion to help her in her work. In reply to her sincere prayer, Lord Shiva appeared as a youthful labourer. He agreed to look after her portion for the small wages—the crumbs of pudding that she would give him.

But the labourer was very playful and sleepy. He did not do his work of throwing sand in the cracks of the bank.

The strange case of this playful truant was reported to the King. The King ordered him to be beaten by his servants. And the boy was beaten, he disappeared suddenly and a wound appeared on the King's body and his servants, nay upon all creatures, both lifeless and with life. They all felt the force of the blow and the mark of the wound. Then, the King realized that he had been foolish in ill-treating such a rare devotee of Lord Shiva as Manickavasaghar. The sorry King then fell at the feet of his ex-minister and begged his pardon. The King placed his Crown, all his riches and his Kingdom at the saint's feet. The saint too was sorry for being the cause for the King to give up all his riches and kingdom. Taking leave of the King, he immediately went away to Uttarakosamangai. He stayed there for some time and composed the "Neethal Vinnappam". From there, he visited various Shiva shrines like Thirupperunthurai, Thiruvaroor, Thiruvidaimaruthur, Thiruvannamalai, Thirukkazhukundram, Seerkazhli, and finally settled down at Chidambaram, as indeed he had been ordered by Lord Shiva.

It was while the saint was spending his time at Thillai (Chidambaram) that he is said to have engaged himself in a debating contest. This debating contest was on behalf of Saivism against the Buddhist monks from Ceylon. What is worse, at the end of the debate, the saint was said to be angry with the Buddhist monks for accepting their defeat. The saint is said to have entreated Goddess Saraswathi to turn the tongues of the monks to dumbness by a curse. That obliging Goddess is said to have done so. Again, at the request of the Ceylonese king, the saint is said to have imparted to the king's dumb daughter the power of answering the doubts and questions about Lord Shiva expressed by the Buddhist monks. Even at the cost of bringing upon oneself the displeasure of some very respectable Saivites, we have to completely ignore and refuse to accept this certain false story which is quite unworthy of the saint and Saivism alike.

After this, one day, an old and venerable Brahmin coming from Madurai reached the Ashram of our saint at Chidambaram. He requested the saint to repeat the whole of Thiruvasagham which the old man took down on palm leaves as it was dictated. Then, at the specific request of the visitor, saint Manickavasaghar sang on the spot another spiritual work of 400 stanzas, called "Thirukkovayar". This is the spiritual classic written on the pattern of nuptial mysticism. This too was written down, by the Brahmin, after which he disappeared.

The next morning, the Thillai three thousand found a big bundle of codjan leaves on the Panchakshara steps of Ponnambalam. When it was looked into, it was found to contain the whole of "Thiruvasagham" and "Thirukkovayar" with these words written at the end: "Written to the dictation of Saint Manickavasaghar by Thiru Chitrambalam Udayan (Lord Shiva Himself)". The astonished priests were asked by an Ashiriree (a mysterious voice—ether voice) to go and meet His favourite devotee, Saint Manickavasaghar living in the north-east end of the town, since he was the author of those works. Accordingly, the 3000 of Thillai went and greeted the saint with all temple honours. They fell at his feet and begged him to explain the meaning and significance of the two works—"Thiruvasagham" and "Thirukkovayar". Silently, the saint went to Ponnambalam. He was accompanied by the Brahmin priests and the band of devotees. As soon as he reached the Panchakshara steps, he pointed with his forefinger to the Lord Sri Nataraja as the meaning of his works. Immediately, there appeared before them the Lord in all His splendour and glory. The saint was not to be found anywhere for he had merged and united with the Lord. The Lord incarnated as Manickavasaghar. He went back from where he came. The devotees gathered there and praised the Lord for this unique vision of the beautification, all on account of the immortal saint Manickavasaghar. They praised the Lord all the more for He was kind enough to grant them such a vision. This is the story of the holy saint Manickavasaghar. Though he had lived only 32 years on this Earth, he is still living through his divine works: Thiruvasagham and Thirukkovayar. They are honoured as the VIIIth Thirumurai in Saivic Holy Hymns. Thirumurai means which makes the devotees to saturate with the Eternal Bliss of Lord Shiva Himself.

Though there are many Krithis and prabandhas in Tamil, Thiruvasagham is an outstanding work which was recited by the Holy Saint Manickavasaghar and it has the Divine Force to make the devotees' hearts get concentrated and merge with the glory of Lord Shiva. Let us also have Holy wisdom of the spiritual peak and thus we make our lives as useful and beneficial. May the Holy Saint Manickavasaghar and Lord Shiva's blessings be showered on all of us!

Om Shivarppanam.

1. Shivapuranam
(Shiva's Ways of Old)

Salutations

Long Live Namashivaya! I offer my humble adorations to the Holy Foot of Lord Shiva.

My humble salutations I offer to the Only One, who does not part from my heart, even for a second which is as brief as the twinkling of my eye.

Glory to the Foot of the Teacher who is a Gem and is ruling in Kokhazhi (Holy Place).

My humble greetings I offer to the Foot of the Only One who dwells very sweetly in my heart, and the One who has become the Agamas.

My praises I offer to the Foot of the One who permanently fills the whole universe and who is the only one and yet not one.

Victory to the Foot of the King who calmed the storm within my soul and made me wholly His own.

Victory to the Holy pair of Feet, which are real jewels, of Pingnakan—the adored Head, Shiva who breaks and cuts away all births.

Victory to the beautiful Feet of Lord Shiva who is far, far away from those who do not love Him.

Victory to the Holy Feet of Lord Shiva adorned with

anklets and in whom those with joined palms rejoice.

Victory to the Holy Feet of Lord Shiva who is glorious and who raises the rank, power and dignity to a higher level, of those who bow their head to adore Him.

Praise to the Foot of Lord Shiva who is also known as Esan. Praise to His Holy Feet who is my father.

Praise to the Foot of Lord Shiva who is the brightest of all. Praise to Lord Shiva's Foot which is shining Red.

Praise to the Foot of Lord Shiva, who is the only one without any stain of sin and the one who always remains deeply rooted in love.

Praise to the Foot of Lord Shiva who is the King and who cuts and breaks away all births which are useless and unnecessary.

Praise to the Foot of Lord Shiva who is our own who, because He dwells in Perunthurai, has made the town glorious.

Praise to the Mountain Kailash where Lord Shiva dwells and from where perfect joy flows in plenty and yet cannot satisfy us.

Introduction

It is Lord Shiva who dwells in my heart, and it is only through that Shiva's kindness alone that He has chosen to dwell within my heart. And I, with great joy in my heart, bow down before His Feet and will narrate in detail Shiva's old ways and how it was only through His own mercy that all my sins of the past have been washed away.

While He is the only one who came to me and showed me His Third eye with kindness and I immediately became speechless and had no time to think, but bowed my head before His Feet which were real jewels, so beautiful.

He is the only one who permanently fills both heaven and earth and yet He is greater and bigger than Heaven and Earth, who cannot be measured.

You are the shining, glorious bright Light and you are the One who has no boundary, but you fill all places and cannot be measured or counted. I am a wicked sinner and I do not know how to sing your praises.

Different Forms

In the cycle of births, I have been born again and again. I have taken different forms in each birth, such as a blade of grass, a herb, a worm and a tree. In my numerous births, I have taken the form of different animals, birds and snakes, I have been born as a stone and as a man, as ghosts and spirits that feed on dead bodies. I have been born as the devils who are mighty. I have taken the forms of wise men and Gods. I have been born into all groups and forms of life which are both movable and immovable. And now, My Lord! in this birth I have become very tired, since I have been born again.

Master is Found

I cannot deny that I have only today seen Your own golden Feet and by this wonderful sight I have come to know what true liberation is!

I find You are the Truth and You live within my soul as the powerful "Omkaram" manthra, through this manthra, You have given me complete liberation.

I have found You to be the spotless One who is without any stain of sin. You own a Bull.

The Vedas call You, Father! the Master and the Guru!

I have found You are hard to analyse or define or perceive or understand. You are in a mysterious way the tallest of the tall and can rise to any height. You are the shortest of the short and can dive deep down to the very depths of the Oceans. You can also expand sideways too.

You are the heat and You are the cold.

You are the ancient soul who is without flaws or defects or mistakes.

You are the true wisdom and its source, You are shining as True splendour also. And out of Your own God will You come to me and made everything that was false in me fly away from me.

I am one who does not possess any knowledge of spiritual mysteries. Even then, You are to me the powerful Lord or perfect happiness.

You are knowledge itself and the source of all knowledge which is good and pure, and so You cured me of my ignorance by giving me knowledge.

Shiva's Five Operations

You have not been created, You are timeless and time does not exist for You. You are without beginning and end, in anything. But, You create all the worlds, which You uphold and protect from falling and then you rub them out by destroying them. And to all these worlds You gave full freedom and Your favour.

You made me enter Your group of servants. Sweet smell can only be sensed by the nostrils. And You are difficult to be perceived or described or understand for You are fine and delicate as the sweet smell which can only be sensed, as it is immaterial.

You are very far away and yet You are very near.

You are the One who is mentioned in the Vedas and still, You are beyond all words and thoughts found in the Vedas.

When fresh milk, cane-juice and ghee are mixed, they rise and become greater. Just so, You spring up and swell with great rank and authority within the hearts of the saints like the mixture of fresh milk, cane-juice and ghee and You dwell in their hearts. You are our Lord who uproots all our births including the present birth also.

Human Form and God's Grace

You are our king and You shine brightly, adorned with the five-fold (Panchavarnam) colours.

When those in heaven sang Your praises You hid Yourself completely, the false sadness and hopeless mood that took hold of me prevented me from singing Your praise.

You had tied me with the rarest cords of virtues and of sins. You had covered the outer part of my body with skin which hides all the worms and dirt inside it.

The cottage, that is, this body with nine doors—outlets, which strongly smell of disgusting dirt, puzzles and confuses greatly the five senses which cheat me. It was all given by You to me who is unimportant and who wilfully continues to do wrong things. And I do not at all have the good qualities needed to unite me with You who has an excited, softened and melting heart, which is filled with love.

You are the purest one.

You came down to this Earth and with kindness showed me Your beautiful Feet which are real jewels.

I was worse than a dog rolling about in the dirt as it were and now, I have become Your slave.

You have come down upon me.

Your Truthful self has, better than even a mother, showered Your mercy upon me.

Words of Praise

You are the brightness itself, which is shaped like a flower which has blossomed out of Light which is pure.

You are shining and gloriously bright.

You are the divine food of the Gods, You are the Lord of Shivapuram.

You are the One most adored and most respected, You break away all the ties of attachments and You guarded me very well.

You dwell within me as the quality of mercy which is like the flood very powerful and flows in plenty without stop.

You showered me with Your loving kindness and drove away cunningness from my heart.

You are the Ambrosia—the Divine food of the Gods. The more, I taste You, the more I want it. I do not get tired or fed up with You. You are the Lord who cannot be weighed or measured.

You are the Brightest light who lives hidden, in a dormant state, within the soul of all. And You keep yourself out of view to those who do not search You.

When liquid is mixed with liquid, it becomes one and cannot be separated. You are the Great soul. You live as the soul of my soul within me. You melt me into liquid which makes me one with You and cannot be separated from You, the Universal soul.

You experience neither pleasure nor pain and You have taken them too, away from me.

You are full of love to those who possess love and who love only You. You are everything and yet nothing at all.

You are the brightness and You are the pitch darkness. Your greatness is veiled.

You are the Beginning, the Middle and the End, and yet, You are not these!

You took hold of me, dragged me and made me Thine own, My Master and Lord You are!

You are the very thought and You are within the thought of those who possess a keen and clever knowledge of the mysterious and with this knowledge understand that you are truly a rarefied and mysterious vision, difficult to be seen.

You are the mysterious understanding and there can be no one who possesses a finer, more mysterious and more delicate understanding than You. You have no entrance nor exit from the world. You do not live in communion with others, but yet, You are present everywhere. You are our Guardian, guiding and guarding us at all the time. You are the Great Light who is a rare sight for our eyes.

Oh! You, My Father, You are the Divine, perfect joy like a stream in flood, gushing down on me.

Yet, You are the visible Light that stands firm and cannot be excelled for You are that magnificent and brilliant light.

No one can judge You correctly for You are the mysterious and finely sensitive power of immediate understanding without reasoning.

Into this world which changes very often You come disguising Yourself in various forms each time you come. And You dwell as the subject of Understanding.

You are the rarest, divine, sweetest food of the Gods called Ambrosia, and You as the Ambrosia, like a spring, You dwell within my heart, My Kind!

Prayer

I cannot any more bear to remain within this mortal human body which is opposite to my wishes and which is disgusting too.

There are those who call You "The Master" and Haran. They pray to You and always live with You by singing Your own praise; their wrong ways have changed to truthful ways, and they shall not any more come back to this earth for they shall have no more births to perform actions which are all just maya. It is only You who can cut away their attachments of the human body, which goes in pursuit of the pleasures of the senses and is deceitful.

You are my Lord who dances well in the middle of the thick darkness.

You are the great dancer within Chidambaram-Thillai. You are the Lord of the Pandyan Kingdom in the South. You cut away the sorrowful births of those who sigh "Oh" unto

You. All those who wish to speak of You find it hard to describe You, for You cannot be described in mere words. But those who wish shall repeat this song, which has been sung beneath Your sacred pair of Feet. And by understanding its full meaning they will reach the sacred town of Shivapuram and humbly bowing their heads in worship they shall stay beneath the Feet of Lord Shiva while all the others shall just pray.

2. Keerthi Thiru Ahaval (The Hymns of Lord Shiva's Renowned Acts)

The Lord Shiva danced within the ancient place of Thillai with his sacred Foot. He is the one who dances within the souls of all creatures. He shines always in all true beauty and his dance has all the qualities of such as grace, excellence and splendour.

You are the Earth, the limitless Sky and the Heavens. You are the richest body of traditions and learning. All these are hidden within You. And by revealing them You have manifested Your true self to us.

You have driven away the darkness of my ignorance in me. It is Your belief and glory to dwell in the house, that is the hearts of saints, which swell with love for You.

You are the one living on the Mahendra Mount. With such grace, You discussed and gave an account of the Agamas (scriptures) which are very ancient. They have already been told by You before. When You were in embrace with Your good spouse. It was at that time when You mingled in love and sweet grace and reached the place of Kalladam (Holy place).

The place of Panchapalli is especially respected because You are associated with it, for You dwell there with Your spouse. Her lips are of red colour and together with Her, in fine milk-words You made known with the sweetest favour, a pool which is close-breasted. This sacred pool does not decrease, but it grows and grows. And You disguised as a hunter, You went down into the pool.

You, the Lord Shiva came dressed like a fisherman and caught a shark from which you brought out the Agamas. You increased the sense of taste by making it sweeter and more agreeable for the Agamas.

Then, You with five-fold face, You explained the Agamas in a pleasing and attractive manner which is endless. You live on Mahendra Mount. And at the sacred place called Nadampadi, You took the form of a sage of the four divine Vedas. You are also the Eternal Aryan who lives and showers true mercy.

You, the Lord, from time to time and age to age, You have changed forms and have taken up different forms and various characters and qualities. You have assumed a crore of shapes and forms.

You are Esan, the Lord Shiva who rides a Bull with a Lady Sakthi who is Your other half, You came to this world and presided over it in order to save it.

In kindness did you go that day with Your fleet of horses which had the beautiful features of the Western Land.

You willingly threw a javelin in the heart of the Velamputhur town and at once a beautiful stream was formed.

At the Santamputtur town, You granted the woman's wish by showing Yourself in a mirror to her.

You, who are very ancient and belong to past times showed, while you handled a horse-gram bag, your beautiful form which is beautiful flame.

Your laws, strength and size were not known to both Vishnu and Brahman. But You did a good deed by changing all the jackals into horses. With Your sacred Foot, You granted me mercy and made me Your slave, You sold all Your horses to the Pandya King. But, You refused to accept the heap of precious gold that was offered to You. In this manner, My Lord! You made him who is Your own.

You made Yourself known to him as the ancient light which persuaded him to follow Your way of kindness and live in the right manner.

You came to me in the form of a wise Brahmin and made me Your slave as a favour You worked upon me Your magic tricks.

Dwelling in the big, worthy city of Madurai, You became a horseman. And then in the very same city, for the sake of withered old woman, Your slave, You were very kind and gracious enough to carry sand for her in a very easy manner. You are the true form of wisdom and residing in the Holy place of Uttarakosamangai You sowed the seeds of true wisdom.

With such charming and beautiful form, You preside over the town of Poovanam. You are as ancient as time immemorial and You revealed Yourself to me in Your simple and chaste form.

You came to Vadavoor and showed Your goodness and love. You were the reason for such sweet music to be heard, because the sweet music produced was the tinkling of Your anklet Feet.

In the wealthy town of Perunthurai, You became the One who is the most generous. You, who are the source of all light, hid Yourself in the radiant Light by Your own cunningness.

In the town of Poovalam, You shone very sweetly. With such favour and goodwill, You wiped out all my sins.

You are the source of all water and very victoriously, You conducted a water-booth and Yourself became the kind water man.

You came as a rare guest too, to the town of Venkadu and on that day, You sat underneath the Kuruntham tree.

By Your own right, You stayed in the Pattamangai town. There, in a way of very pleasing and kindly manner You gave the meaning of the eight mystic powers which is mysterious and beyond our understanding.

You disguised Yourself in whatever form You wished. You took the form of woodman and by Your clever tricks You hid Yourself within the woods.

You assumed all forms that You wished and You took the form that was a fitting One.

You were born upon this Earth as a fine baby, in the town of Oriyur. There, You resided with such grace and was very well pleased. You, then travelled and reached and lived in Pandur. In the beautiful Island, south of Tevur, You took up a royal form.

In the sacred town of Arur, You fasten on to Your body groups of honey-combs. You granted the good people there with knowledge of spiritual mysteries.

When living closely acquainted in Idaimaruthu, You firmly planted Your glittering Feet in that town.

In Ekamban town, You lived with Your spouse—the other half of Your own form—that is, Sakthi, the lady filled with beauty and charm. You lived with her in the most natural way, with all the general and essential qualities of living.

You lived in glory in the sacred town of Vanjiyam. There, You were very pleased to be along with Your devotee, a maid who had sweet smelling locks of hair.

You showed Yourself in various forms. You became a warrior, with a mighty bow in Your hand.

In the Kadambur town, You found a suitable place, where You stayed.

On the Engoi Hills, You showed Your form of sweet beauty.

In the Holy place called Ayyaru, You took the form of a true Saivite.

You dwelt with immense love in the Holy place of Thuruthi.

You dwelt with pure love and kindness in the sacred town of Pannaiyur.

In a vision, You showed Your form in the sacred place called Kazhumalam.

Even now, and without end, You still live on the Kazhukkundru hill.

You taught the townspeople of Purambayam many virtues that cannot be counted.

In Kuttralam, You were a sign that gave evidence and pointed to Your existence.

You hid Your own Fire-like form which is endless and full of glorious charm. But You came as the primitive one of beauty and with a magic and brilliant trick You showed Your grace.

You are the Lord who is full of mercy. To us, You are the Supreme Lord who takes in everyone's qualities and characteristics into Your own self and yet You shine as You alone, the Lord of all creatures.

You came as a Teacher from the Celestial light of Chandradeepam sliding down from the high regions, You reached the beautiful place of Palai safely, and You filled the place full with Your great beauty and perfect happiness.

You dwell on the Mahendra, which is a mighty mountain of Manthra. You are the kind and mighty Lord and Your true greatness has no end.

To tell the manner in which You made us Your own; You in order to draw our attention held up very high the banner bearing stripes of ash which was powerful, sacred and beautifully soft.

In your merciful kindness You gave, in the form of a river, the perfect happiness which is even delightful and which uproots and washed away all my sins and shortcomings.

The beautiful lady who is Your half is very rare for she is full of mercy which is infinite.

Your own Nada-sound which is powerfully loud is the roaring drum that is round.

You handle Your trident—that is the spear with three points with mercy, because, You save and bless all the souls from all the impurities.

You are the One who cuts off all the three fundamental ties of attachments and thus You make us free. Your attractive and beautiful form is the purest, for You are brilliant, glittering, very bright Light and its splendid rays.

You are the first and unparalleled beauty, fittingly adorned with Kazhuneer garlands too.

You are immeasurable, for Brahman and Mal did not know how to measure Your Form and size. But You came on horseback, and by riding on it, You exhibited Your perfect horsemanship.

Through Your kindness and mercy, You granted me the right path to live. So, the cycle of births will not have its influence on me, because You have showed me the perfect path.

The Lord of Pandya is Your Old Kingdom.

True. Saints who rightly worship You belong to You. You made them Your own and placed them on the highest place of perfect happiness. Uttarakosamangai is celebrated as a famous town of the highest distinction because, it is Your home town. Your sacred Name is the foremost one to the God of Gods, since You have granted divine regeneration and inspiring influence to all the ancient Gods.

You ride on a horse which gives great and uncommon pleasure. You drive away ignorance from my soul and You fill it full with Your grace.

You make no difference between big and small, the rich and the poor, the good and the bad, the weak and the powerful. You accept and make everything Your own. You accept equally in the self-same quantity, and degree and length every kind of greatness and all the peoples' goodness and strength.

You called me who is dog-like and made me reach the beautiful community hall within the untainted city of Thillai and You made me completely dependent on You.

Those devotees who followed You all the way, that day, were those who were fit and ready to receive Your blessings. So, they merged and got saturated into You, with Your embrace.

Those who could not reach You, the Guru, threw themselves into burning fire. Some grew quite mad and unconscious; some threw themselves upon the ground and rolled about and cried out loudly; some ran away very fast and fell into the sea and died.

Some were wildly excited and cried out repeatedly on the Lord's name. Thus, they reached His Feet and which saves.

You are a great dancer who make Patanjalai embrace Your Feet as a boon.

Thus, some called on You and talked about You with such religious fervour that they were too weary, because they were filled with joy which prevented them from doing anything further.

While these people stood in deep sorrow, the Lord danced in the bright and gold common hall of "Tiger Town". The common hall of Tiger Town is similar to the high and beautiful Himalayas. You, brilliantly, adorning a celestial smile on Your bright face, when You granted grace to Umai who has sweet and rosy lips, and to Kali who dwells there. You are the Supreme Owner of Mount Kailash which produces mysterious sounds. You entered the bright "Tiger Town" with Your band of saints and sweetly inspiring, You dwell with perfect joy.

3. Thiru Andappakudhi (The Cycle of the Universe)

Shiva's Gross and Subtle Shapes!

The global Units of the limitless Universal Universe! The nature of the Universal Universe is very vast and immeasurable.

If we are to describe their strong growth, mighty height and their beautiful, joining features, then, it is that they are greater and go beyond their number. They are more than one hundred crores.

But, You are the Lord of all. When compared You are so much bigger and they are as small as tiniest dot of atom floating in the Sun's rays streaking through the cracks and narrow openings.

If You need to know a little more, the tribes of Lord Brahman and Lord Mal are the masters of creation and sustentation respectively.

Shiva, You are Time itself who is destruction at the end of every age. But Lord Shiva Himself is not concentrating on these actions. You, the Heat and Light in the Sun, the cold in the Moon, in the mighty Agni, You are the Heat, You pervade the vast Ether. You are the speed of the excellent wind. You are the tasty flavour in the water and the strength of the Universe. Likewise, You are the salient features in a prolonged way, it is limitless. They may be billions and billions in number. But You have put forth everything in their positions. Your mightiness is existing even beyond these too.

The Works of the Supreme!

You are the One who belongs to Time immemorial! You create the creator of all things.

You are the God who guards Vishnu, who is the protector of the creation.

You are the One who hides from us all creations that are preserved.

You are the Lord who is held in highest opinion and is greatly respected, as there is no one else who is above and beyond You, who could have control over all the things that are hidden from us.

All those Gods who stand in a high position as the goal and salvation of the six-fold followers of all six-fold creeds, are only mere unworthy insects when compared with You the Great Lord of all.

It is You who daily gives the quality of brightness and glory into the Sun.

It is You who gives the quality of coolness too, to the shining Moon.

It is You who gives the quality of heat to the great and mighty fire.

It is You who gives the Ether the quality of spreading through and getting into every part of all space.

It is You who gives to the noble wind the quality of movement.

It is You who gives the quality of good taste to the clear and cool water.

It is very clear and understandable that it is You who made the Earth so strong.

It is by Your mercy and kindness and love that You give holy orders for a number of crores of things and a number of lives, everywhere and always, to exist and function, and all within their limit and own, separate places.

Shiva's Qualities

Not only that, but more:
See You are the First One, See You are perfection itself!
You are by Yourself a true equal.

See, You wear upon Yourself the tusk of ancient boar.

See, You wear the skin of a forest tiger around Your waist. See, You wear Ash.

The more I think of You, the more I cannot suffer Your absence. See and finally, I die!

See, You are the sweet sound; that is melody of the sweetest Veena's music.

See, You play a good tune too upon the self-same Veena.

See, You are the highest in authority and rank and are of the utmost importance, value and merit.

See, You are the most ancient one.

See, You are the Greatest One to Brahman and Vishnu who is not known.

See, You are the wondrous One, or Your surpass expectation, experience and are inexplicable, See you are the many, for You are found in all things and creatures.

See, You are the ancient one, but You cannot be described by the mere power of words for You are Timeless.

See, You are too far away in space and time that You cannot be grasped or also understood by even the mind.

See, You are the One who can well be caught within the net of Love only.

See, You are known as the "Only One" for You are without any equal.

See, You become larger and wider and spread out to fill the world's wide area full.

See, You are more difficult to be perceived because, You are finer and more delicate than even the tiny atom, the nature of which is not divisible further.

See, You are Esan who is very great and Your greatness has no parallel.

See, You are the Rarest One among the rarest of the rare group.

See, You spread through and get into every part of everything and You make them grow also.

See, You are the knowledge, so mysterious that You cannot be known from the knowledge gained from books.

See, You are the One who expanded Yourself high above and even below.

See, You are the Only One without any end and without beginning too.

See, You are the One who creates attachments and releases the created attachments.

See, You are all the immovable and the movable things.

By Your Holy orders, You create the Ages—immense period of time—and also destroy them, bringing them to their end.

See, You are Esan who can be attained by everyone.

See, You are Shiva who is unknown to the Gods themselves.

See, You are One who is both female and male still you are the neuter gender also.

See, You are the One whom I see with my very own eyes.

See, You are the most delicious drink one can think of, and blessings as sweet as honey flow like a spring from You.

See, I have seen and experienced the greatness of Your mercy.

See, You placed your rosy Feet on the Earth.

See, I too was saturated consciously that He was Shiva.

See, You made me Your own and gave me Your blessings.

See, You are with Your partner of blue eyes.

See, She is with Herself, that is You and You are with Your self, that is She, and both are together.

The Sea and the Cloud

The good old Sea which gives delight, got changed as the dark and mighty cloud which climbed the sacred hill of Perunthurai. At that time, while the lightning's glittering flashes spread on every side, while the five sensed bondage like a glistening snake flies away in fear, while the depth of hard sorrow hides its mighty head, while the Hibiscus flowers of great beauty shine with splendour, while our own countless births increase like the scarlet flies, while the thunder like infinite mercy roars like the drum, and while the upraised palms in prayer look like the Kanthal flowers the shining torrent rolls on every side and reaches the top of the hill, filling all the whirling distress ponds. The herd of large-eyed stags that were thirsty went to quench their thirst. They drank with widened mouths at the six-fold creed which appeared as ponds of water and their painful thirst was not quenched. So, they restlessly moved away and left the place. Just there the flood flowed through the mighty river and then it rose, moved in circles and whirled with endless bubbles of delight.

The flood dashed against the banks of our mighty bondage and with rising waves smashes and washes off the banks, rooting out the mighty trees of our own two-fold deeds of good and evil which have been increasing from age to age and then, rising it causes the pretty water of grace to flow. Then by building huge dams by means of mountain-sandal trees, it flows through the lakes all filled with flowers of the sweetest honey.

And then it fills and overflows the tank full of smoke of agil on its bank, and with beetles which hum their songs, the good sight of this rising flood is caught sight of with pure delight by the mighty farmers who are saints and who are now sowing seeds of love in their fields of worship, will in future reap the fruits also.

Hallelujahs (Songs of Praises)

Greetings to You such a God so rare, for all the worlds to have.

Salutations to the God who wears a black snake as His girdle around His waist.

Salutations to You, the first one, who presides over the sages who are so rare.

Greetings to You the Soldier who has killed all our fears.

Greetings to You who would daily push us along and make us Your own.

Salutations to You who would wipe away all big sorrows that attack us from all sides.

Salutations to You who would grant to those who reach Your Feet, the most delicious drink and food of the Gods.

Greetings to You who would bend and dance in thick darkness.

Greetings to You who is the lover of the Lady with bamboo-like shoulders.

Hail to You our King who is nothing to those who are the enemies to You.

Hail to You who is the treasure-house of help to the men in need, who love You most.

Praises

Praise to You, our King who was the reason for the poisonous snakes to play.

Praise to You, the Great one who has saturated us with the violent working of Love force.

Praise to Him who would reveal his form that is smeared with ash. In all the four directions, He moves the things that move. The things that are in the lying down position, He lays them down. He holds firmly in position the things which stand up right. You are the ancient One who cannot be described by the mere power of words for You are timeless.

You cannot be seen or understood by the powers of the mind.

You cannot be seen by the sense organs such as the eyes.

You unfold and develop the Elements like the Ether.

Your own glory emanates and rises from You like the fragrance of the sweetest flower. It spreads and fills up every place and leaves nothing out.

You came today so easily and freely and had shown me Your own form; You have made me quite free of this body that will quickly lose freshness and colour.

I praise You the shining, brilliant Being, who came down from Your superior position and rank as the Divine and visited me and stayed with me.

Praise to You who gave me this body which melts in love for You alone.

Praise to You who is like a fountain which gives great delight in my heart.

I do not want this body that cannot completely and thoroughly enjoy the overflowing, perfect happiness, which is You, which spreads and rises in waves.

His Sports of Hiding!

You are hidden in Lightning. Like the golden flame-like flash of bright lightning You shine with such brilliance which overflows and rushes out from heaps and heaps of precious green emeralds and red rubies.

Yet, when the four-faced One came searching for You, You had hidden Yourself well then.

Again, You hid Yourself from those who worked hard in order to approach You. They lived well and were guided on by their bookish learning in their search for You.

You hid Yourself from those who concentrated on You with single-minded Love and so continued to love You even while their friends and relations regretted and got distressed over their actions.

You hid Yourself from those who placed their faith in the principles of the Vedic path and subjected themselves to severe practice to follow in the path.

There were those who tried their best to see You with the influence of their magical and mystical tricks. And You by those self-same tricks hid Yourself from them.

You looked kindly on those who were free of malice and held them firmly with the intensity of Your grace.

You showed Yourself first as a male and then changed Yourself into the neuter gender. Again, You hid Yourself as a bright-browed maid.

You hid Yourself from those who at a very young age had given up their five senses such as taste, smell, sight, hearing and touch, and who had performed rare penances sitting upon the far away hills, breathing and living with their skeleton bodies, and disliking and giving up all enjoyments and pleasures.

You hid Yourself from the minds of those who stood wondering if there is One such as You who exists or not.

Have we seen the "Stealthy One" who had hidden Himself when He was sought after even in the days of old and is sought after even today in the present.

Worship

Oh Lord! You must come and You await the best opportunity to come. You must come soon and dwell here.

And when He comes His Feet should be tied with flowers just freshly gathered and pure.

Come all of you round and round and form a circle around Him, follow Him.

For, He slips away from their firmest grips and hides

Himself from those who cry aloud in the manner filled with violent excitement.

He came and spoke for men like me to hear about His nature. That He is "The Self" and at the same time, the self in all beings, creatures and everything.

He sent forth His clear and loud call and made me come. Out of His mercy, He made me His own and showed me the form of a sage, which is His own beautiful form. He is God who has come in the form of my Guru.

All that time, all the while, my body melted with love that was non-stop, I cried aloud and jumping high, I shouted again and again like the high sounding, rolling waves of the Sea, which rises higher and higher, such was my joy!

And throwing my head first down on the ground, I roared and cried and shouted excitedly.

I fainted like the mad, became unconscious and like the frenzied I just looked fixedly and intently.

People became confused and puzzled; those who heard me were overcome with wonder.

Like the elephant which is affected with rut and burning with mad rage would not allow its mahout to climb on to him, I too was overwhelmed with love and I could not withhold my love any way; while He filled my every part of the body with sweet honey.

Just as He pulled down and burnt the ancient cities of His old, strong enemies, even now with the brightness of His own charming smile and by means of the fire of His own mighty grace, He burnt own humble dwelling places, we, His own slaves and went away leaving nothing intact.

Ecstasy

You have become a Nelli-fruit within my spacious palm.

I do not know what to say, but, I can only offer You, My Lord! My humble adorations.

It is just that I cannot tolerate my dog-like self.

I do not know what You have done to me at all.

Oh! I am dead, Neither do I know what You have in Your mercy done to me, Your slave.

Neither can I drink, taste and experience Your peace and happiness and in this manner rest satisfied. Nor have I the strength to drink it deeply in.

You have made my heart which resembles the violent Sea on a full moon night into a cooling Sea of Milk, rich and sweet in taste and smell. You filled my heart full with the waves of Your Bliss.

You filled the small interstices of my hair-cells full with the flood of sweet ambrosia—the drink of the Gods that is so delightful it cannot be described in words.

This body of mine which is dog-like, You made it Your dwelling place, and You continually supply and nourish every fleshy limb of this body of rough and cruel self, with Your own grace which is like honey.

You filled, drop by drop, the deep holes of all my bones full with wonderful, sweet Ambrosia. While He had blended and mixed in me His mercy which is Supreme honey and while He had also prepared and served His good grace and His ambrosial food to me, He has not made His greatness known even to both Vishnu and Brahman.

4. Potri Thiru Ahaval (Sacred Hymn of Praise)

Lord Shiva's Feet

While the four-faced One Brahman and all the Heavenly Gods bowed their heads down and stood, the tall and beautiful Narayana who is Mal, whose shining crown glitters very well and who had with His pair of Feet measured all the three-fold world. And Vishnu who had been worshipped in all the four directions by the sages, with all their five senses in full perfection, was once all too eager to know where Your Feet ended. And for this reason, He took the form of a mighty male pig and advanced gradually ahead digging out and piercing through the seven-fold under the deep Sea.

He failed to find out, and so, He became tired and cried out aloud, wishing You victory, You, the First of all ages.

Though He had in this manner worshipped You, yet He could not catch sight of Your own pair of flower-like Feet that day. But, which can be worshipped within this world, surrounded by the Sea.

Human Form

They were, from the elephants down to the tiny ants, all

saved from all within the diverse countless wombs of all creations.

Even in this human birth, they have been properly saved from the quarrelling, growing worms within their mother's womb.

In the first month, they escaped from occurring as the twin state when it is the size of a Tandri.

In the 2nd month, they escaped the state of shapelessness.

In the 3rd month, they escaped the state of giddy liquid.

In the 4th month, they escaped the dense darkness.

In the 5th month, they escaped the state of being wiped out.

In the 6th month, they escaped the itching pains.

In the 7th month, they escaped birth by abortion.

In the 8th month, they escaped from congestion.

In the 9th month, they escaped from mental pain, severe pressure and fatigue.

In the 10th month, they and their mothers are still alive and safe after passing through the sea of childbirth and its sharp pain and their sorrows too.

And when they grew up every gear in the manner, they were saved from the evil of earning and storing wealth and also saved from many ills.

They have escaped from all dangers that are hidden in Nature's call in the morning. They have escaped from the dangers hidden in hunger in the afternoon too. They are saved from the dangers hidden in the midnight sleep. They are saved throughout their life's journey.

They have escaped from being enslaved by the passion of the sweet girls whose eyes are sharp, whose curly hair is dark and whose good lips are red. Their teeth are white and their manner of walk is too fine like the walk of the pea-hen in the cool and wintry days. Their breasts that grow close to each other are very tender and their tight fitting garments expand and burst because of their deep heaving. Because they are erect and bright, they grow in size in front and spread so much that their thin waists shrink in pain when they breathe, and in between their two breasts not even a thread can pass through!

They have escaped from living among people who are two greedy for worldly possessions which are not permanent.

Just like a person who escapes with his life from an elephant mad with rage being affected with rut, so too, they have escaped from greed, though living with people who are mad after worldly possessions which are not permanent.

They are saved from the pride of having acquired vast learning on different subjects.

They have escaped from the pains, sorrows and discomforts which wealth brings with it.

They have been saved from poverty which is a very old type of poison.

They have been made to escape from the toil and labour of all kinds of work whose range of action is limited, in every sphere of life.

Sixty Million Beliefs

At that time, the idea of God appeared when the search began for the Highest Being who was the most superior in rank, authority, merit and value and who was free from all passions and who was without an equal.

A battle of cunning and deceit was differently played by sixty million powerful ideas and beliefs about the existence of God.

Trusted friends and neighbours all gathered together and argued that there was no God, till their tongues were burnt with scars.

Friends and relatives, like the ancient herd of cows, came

and caught them and dragged them into further argument and were worrying and complaining on and on.

The Vedicas who were well versed in the Vedas said that penance alone is the supreme and true God. And they quoted from the scriptures in order to prove that their statement was true.

People of every religion argued that their religion alone was true.

Shouting loudly and in a quarrelling manner, Creed, the mighty maya which is an illusion, came like a violent storm and whirled about, rousing their feelings and sentiments and making blasting noises.

The Mighty shining snake of Lokayat (mundane) spat its cruel poison at different stages while the great and varied cheats in these surrounding wells came and got at them, but they did not fall a victim into these.

Successful Conversion

They have caught hold of You in a tight grip and once caught they will not loosen their grip on You. Their heart is like wax which melts when placed before the fire. Their bodies dancing and shouting loud, they worshipped You and cried with trembling.

They sang songs of praise and with bowed heads they worshipped You.

The fools with the tight grip of a pair of tongs did not loosen their victims whom they held very tightly.

They too were filled with unending love which is pure. And just as a soft tree when pierced with a heavy iron rod oozes out water, so too, their softness was seen when their eyes were filled with tears which flowed down in streams.

With melting hearts, they were tossed about like a Sea.

Quite in keeping with these actions, their bodies were trembling, while the worldly people mocked and laughed at them and called these devotees ghouls—meaning spirits who prey upon dead bodies. But the devotees who had given up all their sense of shame did not feel that they were treated with disrespect at the scornful words uttered by the worldly people. Instead they adorned themselves with these disrespectful words as if like a garment.

They lost their sense of active action and so gained the true knowledge of the spiritual mysteries. They were filled with great amazement at the thought of the goal that lay before them.

Just as the cow calls its calf, these devotees shouted and fretted about restlessly calling upon Your Name. Even in their dreams, they thought of no other God, but You.

They did not consider it cheap and disrespectful that the Supreme Being, who is the First One, came, with such a rare greatness and grace, upon this earth as the Great Teacher.

Just as the shadow cannot be separated from the object, so too, the devotees followed Your sacred pair of Feet, behind and in front. They walked in the self-same direction wherever You went, for they had no choice of their own as they had given up desires and hated nothing.

The bones became soft and melted in love. Their hearts became pure, sympathetic and wise by experience and finally dissolved. Their love like a stream overflows its banks. With their five good senses brought under control are concentrated on You alone, they with foolish enthusiasm like madmen, flattering in their words they cried out to You as their Lord.

The hair on their bodies bristled and stood on end, their palms are naturally red folded and closed in worshipping you; their flower-like hearts opened up, their eyes were full of joy and delight due to victory; again their eyes were filled with tears of joy which flows down trickling drop by drop.

Thus, in this manner, the devotees took great pleasure in such a love which cannot be satisfied, grows and prospers continuously.

Praises

Praise to You who like a mother had nursed and brought up all these saints.

Praise to You, Oh Lord who has come as sage to reveal the Truth, I ask to help me do away with the chain of actions in this birth.

Praise to You who are the King of Golden Madurai Town.

Praise to You, the Gem of a teacher of Koodal.

Praise to You, the Great dancer who danced at the court of South Thillai.

I praise You as the Ambrosia which is rare and You are to me today this Ambrosia, the rare and divine food of the Gods.

I praise You, the author of the four great Vedas, who does not become old.

I praise You, Oh Lord Shiva who has a bull-marked banner of Victory.

I praise You, the First One, the fruit who has peeled the fibre from stone.

I praise You, the mountain of Gold and ask You to protect me.

I praise You and ask You to grant me Your grace.

I praise You, the One who creates, protects and destroys.

I praise You who are my father who wipes out all sins and sorrows.

I praise You who is Esan, I praise You who are the Lord over all the things.

I praise You King, You are the Nectar and I praise You.

I praise You who are the Proteus of the fragrant Feet.

I praise You who are the First One and I praise You who are the wisdom itself.

I praise You as You are my salvation, You are the sweet fruit and I praise You.

I praise You, the One who has the origin of a River on Your plait.

You are my owner, I praise You, You are the power of understanding and I praise You.

I praise You as You have chosen me a humble person and kept me as Your slave.

I praise You, Oh Guru, I praise You as the Atom.

I praise You Lord Shiva, You are the Chief, I praise You, You are the sign and symbol, I praise, You are my thought, I praise!

I praise You who are the rare nectar of the Heavenly Gods.

I praise You, the one who is easy to be addressed by everyone.

I praise You, Oh King who gives grace to save all the three-fold relations of seven generations from their sufferings and raging hells.

I praise You, my friend, You are my help and I praise You.

I praise You who are ever free.

I praise You who are the source of all living things.

You are the Father of all, so I praise You, You are Haran, I praise You.

Praise to You who are without an equal beyond words.

Praise to You, the one who is beyond the range of all knowledge and sight.

Praise to You who are the yield and the harvest of those living in a world surrounded by Sea.

Praise to You who are of simple beauty among all the rarest things.

I praise You who are the pupil of my eye which has the colour of dark clouds.

Praise to You who are the living mountain of Sacred Grace.

You are the great warrior who has made even me Your

slave and has placed Your Feet upon my head, I praise You.

Praise to You who wipes away all sorrows of those who come to You, with palms raised in prayer.

Praise to You who are the Sea of bliss, which does not dry up.

Praise to You who has no death and no birth, for You are beyond these occurrences.

Praise to You the source of all, the First One who surpasses everything else.

Praise to You who are like a mother to all those angels who dwell in Heaven.

Praise to You who spreads out as the fifth element in Earth, and as Earth.

Praise to You who runs as the fourth element in Water.

Praise to You who shines as the third element in Fire.

Praise to You who delights as the second element in Air.

Praise to You who grows as the first element in Ether.

Praise to You who are the Ambrosia of my heart which melts.

Praise to You who are difficult to be seen by the Gods, even in their dreams.

But You have blessed my dog-like self with the vision of Your glorious self even in my dreams and also while I am awake, and I praise You.

Praise to You Father in Idaimaruthur.

Praise to You who carried the Ganges River in Your Plait.

Praise to You, the King who dwells in Arur.

Praise to You of famous Ayyaru.

Praise to You of Annamalai and who is honoured by everyone.

Praise to You, Our Father living in Ekambam.

You are the Supreme One, who lives in Paraithurai and so my humble praises to You.

Praise to You Shiva who dwells in Sirapalli.

I do not have any other support except You. So, I praise You who are my only support.

Praise to You, Our dancer, in Kuttralam.

Praise to You Oh King, who lives in Kokazhi.

I praise You, Oh Father, of the Engoi Hills.

Praise the most handsome One of proper pazhana.

I praise to You the self-born who revealed Yourself of Your own accord in the Holy place of Kadambur.

Praise to You, Father, who are gracious to those who surrender themselves to You.

Praise to You, Oh King who blessed and helped the six persons and the elephant, who were under the Ethi Tree.

Praise to You who are Lord Shiva of the southern land.

I praise You the Lord of every land.

I praise You who out of Your grace fed the piglets with milk.

I praise You, the grandest One who is dwelling on Mountain Kailai.

Praise to You Lord, who is like a mother to grant me grace.

I praise You to grant me the thirst to be merged eternally with You.

I praise You to bless me and tell me not to be afraid of anything, for You are with me always.

Praise to You who drank poison as one would drink honey.

You are my father, I praise You as You are my teacher.

You are the Eternal One who has no End, I praise, You are the spotless One without any stain of sin, I praise You.

I praise You, Oh! Beautiful lover.

I praise You Oh! Bhava.

Praise to You, Oh! Great One.

You are the Lord, I praise.

Praise to You, the Rare one.

Praise to You, the purest one.

I praise You who are the beautiful path to the vedic saints.

I cannot bear it, Is it Just, Praise to You the First One.

Praise to You who are my relative, You are my life and so I praise You. You are glory. I praise, You are Shivam. I praise You.

I praise You the most handsome. You are the Bridegroom, so I praise You.

I am Your slave and my dog-like self is burdened with mental agony, but I praise You.

You are my eye of Kavaithalai and I praise You. You are the King of the Holy Hilly lands.

Praise to You of cultured Arikesari.

Praise to You the Richest one of Thirukkazhukkundram.

I praise You, the Haran of Hill like Poovanam.

I praise You who are without form and yet with form.

Praise to You who is a mountain of mercy.

Praise to You, the glorious light who passes through and goes beyond the range of "Thirumayam".

Praise to You who are the clear knowledge of spiritual mysteries and yet, it is very difficult for me to know and understand You.

Oh! You are that admirable and gorgeous reflection of radiance from the perfect pearl, and I praise You.

Praise to You who are love itself and the object of love to Your own slaves.

You are Grace and that wonderful drink of the Gods called Ambrosia, which cannot satisfy one.

I praise You, the One who is called by a thousand names.

I praise You who are adorned with Taliaruhu garland.

Praise to You the dancer of Light which increases and grows.

You are the beautiful Lord of sandalpaste and so I praise You.

You are the One who dwells on the Mighty mystic mountain of Kailash, and so I offer You my praise.

You have wished to accept us as Your slaves, to save us from all dangers and so, I praise You.

I offer You my praise, for You in Your kindness and mercy made a tigress feed upon the breast of a deer.

You are the One who walked upon the violent waves of the Sea.

I bow down in praise to You who showed kindness on that day to the tiny black-bird.

I praise You who dwell in me and help me kill the five senses, You are worthy of praise, for You walked upon this earth in different forms.

You are the bottom, the middle and the top and so, I praise You.

You, in Your kindness and mercy gave to the king of Pandya the highest salvation which was neither hell, nor heaven nor even earth, I praise You.

You are the One without empty space anywhere fills all things, I praise You.

You are the King of Shivapuram, very rich in flowers and so, I praise You.

You are God who wears Kazhuneer garlands and so, I praise You.

Praise to You who breaks away all false beliefs and vain hopes of Your worshippers.

My dog-like self which is worthless, does not know anything of right and wrong, but I have today wreathed a garland in words like flowing liquid. And may You, My Lord accept it and bless me, and You are worthy of my humble praise.

Praise to You the Ancient One who burnt forts in plenty. You are the magnificent brightness, who is greater than the greatest One and so, I praise You.

I praise You, the serpent wearing Lord. I praise and praise You who are the Ancient cause, origin and God. Praise to You, Praise to You, Victory to You, Victory and Praise to You again and again!

5. Thiruchatthakam (The Sacred Cento)

1. UNSHAKABLE FAITH (WONDROUS SPIRITUAL STEADFASTNESS)

1. Knowing the Truth—Humble Approach to the Master

My body is excited and so trembles before Your sweet scented Feet. I raise my hands above my head in worship, with folded palms. My eyes are filled with tears. Everything that is false and untrue flies away and vanishes from my melting heart, as You are dwelling within. My tongue will not give up praising You and shouting Victory to You repeatedly. So, I praise You, accept my Lord.

2. Self-surrender and Firmness

I would not recognize or even accept the posts or state of Indhra, Vishnu or Brahman, when You have accepted me. Though my house is destroyed, I will be a friend to none but only to Your own saints. I will not hate Hell but will readily accept to go there, even if it is Your will to place me there. You are our King and above everyone. So, I would not think or worship any other God except You.

3. My Wish

Thinking of Your Feet, my noble Lord and Guru, my heart melting and I talking in a simple way as a child about things that suits my violently excited soul, walked from place to place with no specific destination that one might call me mad. They speak out all that their minds do think of me, and I ignore talk like the dead. When will that day dawn?

4. The Rude Shamelessness of Devas

The Lords of Creation, Sustentation and Destruction—Brahman, Vishnu and Rudhra took part in Dakshan's sacrifice and happily consumed the flesh. They were punished by Sri Veerapadhra. When the milky Sea was churned, they enjoyed with pleasure the worthy outcome. But when the mighty poison came out, they in fear of death simply cried out to Shiva as Father to save them. Since they too suffer the joys and sorrows of the Universe; they too are considered to be as ordinary as human beings!

5. My Vain Birth

I have not performed any penance, not have I freely worshipped You with cool flowers, without limit. And because of cruel fate, I have been born in vain. I have not attained the knowledge of spiritual mysteries which give release of the soul from the body and which are the possessions of Your saints. My Lord of Lords! grant me, Your slave, the birth to reach Your Holy Feet.

6. I want perfect love to pray

You are One who plays tricks and You are not easy to be found, but You do not hide from the hearts of saints, who roam and worship at Your Feet with different and uncommon flowers without limit, and hope to be blessed with all that they prayed for. Grant me perfect love to see Your Great Feet to praise You forever.

7. Shiva's Greatness and Simplicity

Brahman, Creator of all the worlds and who is the father of them all, had once before searched, to see Your Holy Feet. But You went beyond His knowledge and sight and did not make Yourself known to Him. And now, You, here, dance on this cremation ground with spirits. You wander like a mad man with violent excitement, without friends and dressed in tiger's skin.

8. Lord Shiva is Eternal!

When will the time come for the five elements such as the wandering wind, fire, water, earth and the Ether to merge with nature at the time of the Great Destruction. Oh Father! the mighty Time which can construct and conduct the creation and the destruction, which was mastered by You. You are the Mahakala to destroy my dense sins. Save us from the sufferings of sins and Time!

9. May the Lord as Glorified!

Our Lord Brahman is God Shiva who is the King of Heaven. The wreath of His Crown is the great, cool Moon. Though He knows and has seen my unworthiness too, yet, He has made me His own, I announce that He is my Lord and that I am His slave, so that the world might know my Lord's Greatness.

10. His Laugh-provoking Sport!

I am not fit to enter into the company of Your saints. You are my perfect Gem. You are my Father and You are as sweet as Honey. Was it just that You should make me Your own? You raise the rank and dignity of those who are poor

and lowly and You heighten their state of spiritual delight.
So also You degrade the heavenly ones. Our Lord, I cannot
understand You for what You have done is a laugh-provok-
ing Sport!

2. INTRODUCTION (ENLIGHTENING THE MIND)

11. I want Perfect Love!

Just as one plays a part on the stage, I too pretended the
part of Your own saint and ran in the company of Your saints,
with great speed to enter heaven. You are a bright mountain
of Gems on Gold; My Lord in Your kindness and mercy,
please grant me that for never-ending love for You, which
would melt my heart.

12. I want nothing but Your Grace!

I do not at all have any fear of births; I do not care about
death even. Even if Heaven is given to me I do not want it.
I do not hold dear the earthly riches and crown. Oh Shiva of
Cassia flowers which are as sweet as honey, You are my Lord
and Father too. I cry to You in pain asking when the day will
come which brings Your mercy.

13. I uncared for!

With my dog-like self, I who am Your slave, have a
strong desire to see Your Flower-like Feet. I do not decorate
or adorn Your Feet with flowers, but I wait on You and sing
words of praise till my tongue gets bruised and scarred. You
who had bent the golden Mount, should You not grant me
Your gracious Nectar? I will in an unhappy state feel deep
sorrow. I will be uncared for. What will my fate be then?

14. I hurry to my ruin!

My heart does not soften nor does it melt in love to reach

Your Feet. I do not worship nor do I praise You. Oh King of Gods, I do not even adorn You with wreaths of flowers. I do not sweep or even clean the temple where You preside. I do not dance, but hurry to my death, that is ruin. But You will reach me through Your own skill.

15. God is All!

You are the sky and the earth. You are the wind and the fire. You are the body and the soul. You are the living beings and the non-living beings. You are the King at whose command You cause everyone to dance like puppets, and it is only You who have the right to use these words of egoism like—"It is I and this Mine". What words shall I speak and how shall I praise You, I do not know.

16. The Gods' Prayer and Mine!

The Gods praise You only because they want to prosper, They pretend modesty before You, So that, they may be exalted and worshipped. You have garlands around You at which bees keep humming. I am Your slave who is dog-like and I praise You that You may cut away my worthless births which are yet to come.

17. Will Your servants see more of You!

The Heavenly ones praise You and the four-fold Vedas sing Your praises. Your spouse with locks of Kura flowers is sharing half of You. Your saints who love You truly group themselves together. Oh Rare One! can all of them see more Your pair of Feet with anklets.

18. My Soul cannot Endure!

It is too difficult for everyone to know and analyse that You are moving in a very mysterious manner in Ether-space. You are our Great One of the Ambalam. I take refuge beneath Your jewelled Feet which my poor self has made its own. I do not shower sweet flowers nor do I cry with amazement and melt. I cannot suffer any longer. What is the next step? I wish to die!

19. God's in His Heaven I pray Not!

Oh! My mind which is ruined pants and yearns and melts for cupid's flowery arrows of spring. It yearns in lust for the maidens with white teeth, red lips and painted eyes. So, You do not see Him who has taken form and has come to the Earth and dwells here even now. You just ignore Him. Is it not better to die than live in this melting flesh, by not seeing Him.

20. Oh Mind! Beware of Your Ruin!

Oh, My mind that is living a soulless life; because of your cruel fate you are sinking. you are not singing in praise of Him who would save you from sinking in ruin. I have warned you very often, and yet you plunge yourself always into the flooded Sea of sorrows.

3. DYING TO SENSE AND SELF

21. My Cold and Hard Heart

Your locks of hair are only broad and plaited, and then from where does the water rush in and flood? You who ride a bull, Those who heard these words, that You are the Overlord of the Heavenly Ones, fell in love with You and tumbled upside down, like a mighty flood which runs down violently into a big bottomless pit. And I was standing near with trembling hands and melting heart, You came to make me Your own. But my human body like a heart from head to foot did not all melt and become soft. My whole body just as one eye did not flood with tears. Oh Lord! so my heart is made of stone and my pair of eyes, of my sinful body, which has dried up, is made of the hardest wood only.

22. I am a steel puppet

You came before me and asked me to come to You for You were the One who slays my sins. Thus, You entered my own soul which was wrapped up in sins, You announced Your coming and made Your abode in me who is Your slave. Thus, You became my Lord. But yet, I am a puppet, and that too a puppet made of steel, for I did not at all sing Your praises, nor did I stand and dance in extreme joy; I did not cry loudly, nor did I dry up; I did not even faint and fail my soul. Oh, You are the ancient one. Is it that I have become quite meek? You are the First One and the Last One. I beg You to tell me, for I do not know how all this would end.

23. God's Generosity

Although, I had known well that You are one of the Four Vedas and though I had seen and known that I am the meanest one of all and simply I had cried to You, Oh Lord! for I was too full of love for You. And You had accepted me a dog-like one as Your own. Are there not enough of saints for You to choose, than I, with my evil self which is a spirit? Ah! this shows Your greatness which is so rare. Oh! My Lord with what words shall I speak of this?

24. How Wondrous Your Grace!

Whenever they spoke, they spoke again and again of You. Oh! Esan, as mother, father and mighty Lord whenever they smeared themselves, they smeared themselves fully with plenty of sacred ash. They cried with constant love praises to You, shouting that You were their Great King, in all their cycles of births and deaths. Oh You, Our father, You have made them all Your own. And You are the flawless mount of gems. Finally, You made me as one who is full of lust and full of cunning. Even so, You have made me Your own servant now. All this is very amazing and surprising!

25. God's Manifestations!

Your true colour is neither red nor white. You manifest Yourself as all beings, and yet You are one. You are the smallest atom and yet, the one who is difficult to be perceived or described, because You are too fine and delicate, as You are mysterious. Thus the heavenly company is confused in their thinking, for they do not know how to reach Your Feet. But Father, You did show Your colour, Your form and Your flowery anklet Feet to me.

26. Consecration of My Body

The thought of my own dog-like self, You filled full with thoughts of You alone and You filled my pair of eyes with the splendid sight of Your Flowery Feet. You have also accepted and allowed my humble homage reach Your Feet. You have made my tongue sing Your praise with ruby-words. You have made me feast my senses, for You came and entered into me. Then, You made me Your own. Oh! You are a mighty Sea of magic for I cannot understand You. You are the Ambrosia—the rarest and delicious drink of the Gods, and Oh! You are the mount. You are a rare and beautiful sight for Your form, which is like red lotus flowers growing thickly together, has no equal to it. You gave me Your Self, to me who is a lonely person.

27. The Raft of Five Letters!

When I was unhappy and forsaken, I was tossed upon the big rolling waves of great sorrow, within the mighty Ocean of the births. At that time, I did not have anything to hold on to, nor did I have a single support. Again, when maids who had red, fruit-like mouths, came like a violent storm and whirled about me, I was caught between the jaws of lust which is like mighty shark; at that time, I thought and thought very often as to the ways I should seek, in future, in order to be released. And then I caught hold of the raft of the five mystic-lettered sound—NAMASHIVAYA and floated on the waves. Oh! You are the ancient One, and You revealed to me who is a wicked soul, a place of safety and rest which is fertile and which has neither origin nor end.

28. Celestial Vision and Sounds!

No one can ever come to know You through the words heard from others used in order to describe You. You do not have even the least sign of decay and destruction. You do not have friends and relatives. You have heard all things and so You know everything, even though You have not directly heard anything with Your physical ears, for You are omnipresent. Oh Lord! You have worked such wonderful deeds which are like magic, because when the people of the town were keeping watch, waiting for You, You offered me, who is dog-like, in this world a sear of honour. And to me who is a dog, You manifested such a glorious vision that was not shown before to anyone, and made me hear magnificent sounds that were unheard of and not heard before. You made me Your own by giving Your self to me and saved me from future births.

29. Wonderful Grace!

A person asked if there was even anyone who had seen such work which was so wonderful. It was because of Your Holy Grace and mercy, You made me the servant of Your great saints who were with great love for You. You had also wiped away all my fears and had made me Your own slave. You had unseemingly entered into me by merging Your Self with my self, thereby making me Your own. While my heart which was like a spring of nectar melted and my love for You increased and swelled up. You who are my master was male, female and the neuter gender and the fire, all at the same time, You are the end. I cannot place You within a boundary saying, You are this and that, for You go beyond all these things and stand out with a form which is like crimson flowers. You are our own Shiva. You are our Lord, as well as asking of all the worlds.

30. We Fear Nothing!

You are the God of Gods and unknown to even the King of Gods. You are the Lord of the three, who all the fertile worlds create, preserve and destroy. You are outstanding for You stand forth as the First One, that is, the ancient one. The forms of all the three are Yours. You are the master of masters. You are our own Father whose other half is ruled by the lady, Parvathi. You, the Lord of all, have made me Your own. Hereafter, we are not slaves to anyone else. Nor are we afraid of anything. We have reached the servants of Your saints and we shall more and more engage ourselves in activities for amusement and fun. We shall play with great joy.

4. SOUL PURIFIED!

31. Oh! My Deadened Mind

Oh! My Mind, You do not dance and You do not have love for the Feet of the Dancer (Lord Shiva) who danced at Thillai. You do not sing with the melting body. You no longer tremble, nor do you bow in respect, Oh! Mind that is dead, you do not cajole with His Lotus-petal like Feet and place them on your head, nor do you deck them with flowers. You go crying through the streets, but you do not search for Him. I do not know what is to be done next.

32. My Perverse Mind

You are the Universal self and You have entered into me who is ignorant, without knowledge, You merged Your self with my self and enlightened me with true wisdom of the self. You had shown me all the higher paths to realize You who is the Universal consciousness. You are the master who has blest me with blissful grace which is changeless and You break all my bonds of attachment and desire. But, Oh Mind, You are still blindly wrong, a mind which is dead. Because of Your increasing lies You disgrace and like a devil, you send me to my ruin.

33. I cannot brook my mind

Oh! My stupid and senseless mind, I cannot tolerate You any longer as You are obstinate and still do wrong. You are the cause of my destruction. Hereafter, we will not trust you anymore. Although, You saw bright ash on the huge shoulders of Lord Shiva, You did not make my body melt, nor did you make me tear it. It is Your nature to be destructive and I cannot even bear its name.

34. The Folly of my Frivolous Mind

Oh! My mind which I hate so much, You are mischievous too and You should know that the Lord is my master who is great and who had the right even to sell me. I am His own dog-like slave and He is the Lord and Master over me. You have all the pleasures of adoring and worshipping His flower-like shoot of Feet and You in Your foolishness has given them up. Instead, You have been entertaining and enjoying worldly pleasures which are not permanent. Oh Lord! I cannot imagine or even describe in words Your Supreme Wisdom and Greatness.

35. Insensible to Infinite Mercy

Oh mind! You do not realize that My Lord and Master has broken away all ties of attachment and bondage and that He dwells there. You do not melt in love for Him; You do not hate all your sins, and thus, have not built a huge mansion for Him in your heart. You are unaware of His mercy which is endless, for His mercy is much needed for your good and for your release from everything. You do not bow in respect and worship, paying homage to the master's feet which cleans the dirt from the mind.

36. What can I do?

You are fortunate enough Oh, mind to gain the opportunity to give up all your attachments and bondage of this worldly life and pleasures, and reach that Golden city which has no exit but entrance alone. So, there is no chance to come out, but melt with pure love before His Feet, my master and Lord who has made me His own by abiding in me and what will I even do if it were denied to me to taste the Ambrosia, milk and honey?

37. My Iron and Flint Heart

There are no sinners like me, but my Lord, You have not the slightest will to part from me, your dog-like ward. And yet, I parted from Your Feet—the Princely Feet. My mind is as hard as iron and my heart is harder than flint, knowing all this, I have not banged my heart in sorrow. I do not know what my ear is like!

38. Won't I die?

Your nature is not known to all the rest who desire not to reach You, and who are not Your followers. But to those who search for You, You are the Honey, Cow's ghee and sugarcane juice to them. And You are Lord Shiva, the Universal consciousness and the Lord of Shivaloka. And You who have seated on Your right Your most beautiful consort with deer-like eyes, I have failed to acknowledge and thereby ruined myself. I live, and for a long time, I have been nourishing and looking after only my body which is perishable. It is better to die than remain ignorant of You. Oh! When will I die?

39. I shall live!

I have been given the vision of His flowery feet which are brilliant and glittering. His feet cannot be compared and they cannot be measured for they have no limit to end. He gave me such a vision and showered me with the righteous path to attain Him, who is inferior than even a dog. He gave me love which is sweeter than even a mother's. But in order to see Him who is the Supreme consciousness, I am ready to leap into the fire, or drown into the depths of the Sea and even to roll down from the hills to see my King, whom I have failed to see!

40. I revel in my fleshy frame!

I did not take notice of the moon's scorching wounds which cupid's arrows had caused. The curd is churned by the rod. Just like the curd which is churned by the rod, so too, I am caught also in a net and stirred by the deceitful maidens who have eyes like deer. I have not taken steps to go to the city of Shiva who has granted me His grace which is sweeter than honey. I just drag on, only feeding and clothing this fleshy body in order to live, little forgetting that it is perishable.

5. GRATITUDE

41. My Gem! I have seen You!

A twin-trunked tusker though so big in size is not worthy of seeing You. Just like him, I could not see You who are the gem, most precious of my soul, because I am experiencing only sorrows about which I am greatly concerned. You, the Lord of Heaven, who is the Universal consciousness, had called me to enjoy Supreme Bliss. I did not come because I was absorbed in enjoying the worldly pleasures.

42. Optical Illusions?

Those who only by bookish knowledge know that You are the Bright Supreme Being, do not know whether You are a male or female or an eunuch. But to me, Your slave, You have manifested Your true form. Even though, I have seen Your true form, I still remain in the state as if I have not seen You. Have my eyes deceived me or is it just disbelief or intoxication?

43. When can I see You?

Your form has no likeness or equal. Your form is not known even to the heavenly ones. Oh! Dancer, You have made myself Your own, by merging Your Self with me. You are the Earth, You are the Sky and You are the Time—past, present and future—when all these come and go. Oh Lord! I am yearning, when can I be blessed with the vision of Your True form—the Supreme Light?

44. I cannot leave this body

You are the Supreme One who can be understood and seen through only the perfected eye, that is, the celestial eye. Your real form is the One Truth which is like a flame of gorgeous light, dwelling so far away from the mere sight of the physical eye. Like a fledgeling, that is, a young bird, which has just learnt to fly, I too just try to fly away from this earth, leaving my deceitful body which is perishable, and take refuge in You. But I am unable to leave this fleshy body (frame) and merge with You.

45. My Perverse Creed

I have tremendous love for You and I desire to praise You. But calling on Your Holy Name, rolling on the ground with frenzy, standing up and praising You and crying for You, I am unable to do, because my beliefs and opinions are just the opposite to my desire to praise You. My beliefs and opinions are like those of the God of death, who came face to face with You in hatred and finally fell at Your Lotus Feet, because He was defeated.

46. You are Permanent!

Even though small, there is oil hidden in a sesame seed. Just like the oil which is unseen in the sesame seeds, You, my Father are unseen by us; are present below, above, in the middle and in the rest of the things. You pervade everywhere as You are hidden in everything, for You are omnipresent, Will You, who are wearing cassia flowers full of honey and the bees humming around it, call my worn out, feeble self amongst Your saints and make me Your own.

47. He entered my soul!

You are my father, mother and Lord. You are the father, mother and the Lord for all living things. But You are not blest with these three relationships. You are the blessed one whom the mind cannot perceive, understand and even know, for You are the Supreme consciousness. But He had Himself made His entrance within my soul before.

48. I saw Him but left!

Although I have described Him in a very good manner, I have not yet united with Him, but instead I have parted from the boundless jewelled Feet of the Great Being who is rare. He is unknown to both alike, the rich and the poor, He is also unknown to the heavenly Gods, to the worms and grass. It is great sorrow for me with a stone heart to have seen Him and to have then left Him.

49. How I am honoured!

I do not know my numbers. I do not know "Eight and Two" and yet You have cut off all my attachments and bonds to this earthly life, and You have made me Your own servant. You have often placed me upon the public stage so that I can join Your company of saints smeared with sacred ash, and that the other men could see and stare at me in wonder and surprise.

50. I was chosen but not for my wisdom!

You are the Form of Wisdom, the All-wise One. You are the food of the Gods called Ambrosia. Was it because I should be known and called a wise man, that You chose me and made my dog-like self Your servant. Before You entered me, I was ignorant and did You not know of my ignorance and idiocy on the day when You chose me. And now, I do not know whether I am wise or still ignorant. Oh! Esan, Grant me grace!

6. MYSTIC EXPERIENCE PURIFIED!

51. I know not what to do!

Oh! My Esan and My Lord, You are my Father who is great and the only one who can destroy my cycle of births and deaths. Look at me! A wicked dog, rascal and coward, I do not think of You who made me Your own. Before You, I am good for nothing at all. Oh! You are the Bright Lord of Light of the Golden Court. I do not know what to do!

52. I am as unworthy as sinners!

I am a mean dog and I do not know what to do. I am fit to gain all the gifts attained by all the false worshippers who do not know and have not seen Your Flowery Golden Feet. Though I have seen and heard of how Your true, worthy and innocent saints have reached Your sweet Flowery Foot, I remain here still ignoring You, feeding and clothing my body which is mortal, Oh! You, the fearless Lion-hearted warrior destroy my ignorance.

53. Still I die not!

You are the Lion-hearted warrior who left Your Golden city and drove away the darkness too. The glorious saints have reached Your Feet because they have been blessed with grace by You and Your consort who has soft and tender breasts. After seeing this, should I roam about like a blind village hog here. There is no necessity for me to live anymore without Your vision. Will not my cruel, hard self die soon?

54. Your special grace for me!

Great saints and sages have become disappointed because of the mortification and penance they had performed by going beyond and overcoming their bodily passion, for an endless period of time in order to gain vision of Your Form. But You have conquered me a sinner who has taken no pains and have made me Your slave. And I do not wish to throw away this dirty and foul-smelling body, but cling to it ignorantly. My Lord! I am lacking that pining Love to see You. With whose help shall I rise?

55. Yet, I guard this worm house!

The deer-eyed Lady Umadevi is Your half. You are Shiva and the King of south Thillai. You manifested Your self as the honey, the ambrosia and the cane-juice for Your devotees and proved to them that it is only by tasting You and by following the path You have shown, they can reach Your Holy Feet. But I am earth-bound and stay and linger here, left to safeguard this fleshy body which is a house for worms.

56. Is it Your Ordain?

Oh! Master, You are the owner of those saints who have mighty love for You and whose hearts melt in thoughts of You alone. Seeing though the saints who have reached Your sacred Feet, I who am meaner than a village dog did not get thrilled, nor did my heart which is made of stone melt. Is it that You have destined me to guard and look after this foul-smelling, fleshy body which houses worms? It is my ignorance that I live on here and be earth-bound.

57. I succumbed to Maya!

It is proper that will has destined forms. Although I had known how You held Your saints firmly lest they should fall off. I am guilty for I gave myself upto wrong notions and illusions and watched slyly and closely quivering lips, the slight loosening of the dress and tiny drops of perspiration on the maid's face here. By doing this, I have worked upon my own destruction.

58. He will laugh at me but would grace!

He is that Supreme Light and Ecstatic joy which is like

honey, milk and essence of cane-juice, to those who have a mature, realized mind and vision. He is the Heavenly Lord who melts their bodies, I am a worthless wretch and if I should say to Him, You are Mine and I am Yours! He may laugh and disappear and yet bestow His own Grace. And that is my nature!

59. No other refuge for me!

My Lord! Your nature is not known to others; even those who love You do not know Your true nature. But will You, Oh! My Master who made my mean and dog-like self Your servant, make me ever part from You. Who will then look after me? Oh! Mighty King what can I do? Oh! Father of bright, golden Form, if You discard and disown me, where shall I find refuge?

60. My shameless self!

Previously, I have stood amongst Your saints who were praying, and I, a shameless dog, have very proudly and boastfully admired the strength and beauty of my shoulders and felt very delighted. But I lack that melting love which Your saints have, to have your vision. In this state, I ask myself if I am worthy to be even Your slave? Oh My Father! what nature is mine? I doubt my own nature. I cannot tolerate my own lowly and mean nature. I want to reach Your Feet which are my very own.

7. COMPASSIONATE MERCY

61. I cannot brook this frame!

I cannot anymore bear to live this life in this flesh. Oh Sankara! Save me! Oh! You are the Old and the New combined of the Heavens, save me. You are our strong One, save me. You, the unparalleled One, I beg to save me. Save me!

Oh Lord of the Heavenly Ones. Save! Save me! You, the great dancer of Thillai, Our spotless One, save me, please save me.

62. Ecstasy!

You are the Form and sound of the Holy Manthra "Om Namashivaya". I cry to You the serpent wearing Lord for I faint. I praise you *'Om Namashivaya'* for there is no other place or person for me to take refuge, except You. So, do not drive me away from You. Praise and victory to You for conquering me.

63. All in all!

I praise You as the benevolent One because You have blessed me and have made me, who is false and full of deceit in the heart, Your own. I offer praise to Your sacred Foot. Oh My Lord! I praise and praise You again, Like a great flood is Your mercy which is fresh and as Honey, Oh! save me, Lord! You are the five elements—Earth, Water, Wind, Fire and Sky. You are the Moon and the Sun and also the individual soul.

64. Rid me of this body!

I praise You, Oh God, look at my unworthy self and give me grace. I pray earnestly that this poisonous heart of mine be melted and removed by You. I pray that You quickly strip away this body frame and kindly give me an abode in Heaven. I praise You, Oh Sankara! who has placed the Ganges River on Your plait. Again and again, I praise You.

65. I cannot live anymore!

I praise You whose own half is Lady Uma Devi of Red mouth, white teeth and bright painted eyes. I praise You, the Rider of Mighty Bull. Oh Sankara! I plead to You that I have no other refuge, except You. My Lord! I am greatly disgusted with living on this earth, and hate this body. I cannot bear to live any longer.

66. Pardon my sins!

I am disgusted for I am the cause of my own ruin, and so I praise You, but have myself. I do not blame You. But instead, I praise Your Holy Feet which made me Your own. I praise You, for You are novel and it rests in You to forgive all our faults. My Lord! I praise, who rules the heaven. I praise You the One who gives liberation from this earthly life. So end this life of mine soon.

67. Adoration

Praise to You, Lord, who is like a Lion to all the heavenly ones. You are the partner of Lady Umadevi of slender waist. I praise the One who wears white, sacred ash. Praise to You the Red hued Lord and You, the Lord of Thillai's sacred court. You, Lord of Heaven I praise Only You are my master. I have no other than You to give me salvation.

68. Destroy my loneliness!

You are still unique, though You manifest Yourself in several ways and forms. Praise to You master who cannot be compared. To all the heavenly ones, You are the Teacher. Praise to You, Komala's tender shoot. Accept me as Your very own, for You call me to come to You, strengthen this bond. I praise You to grant me the vision of Your Foot and save my lonely, helpless self from this earthly life.

69. You, the Greatest oft!

Your saints have great love for You. But You have greater love for them, than they have for You. By Your greatness, You have scorched all my lies and falsehood. Instead

You have given me Truth and made me Your own. While You generously drank poison, You gave nectar to the heavenly ones to drink. Grant me the vision of Your Foot and unite my poor, dog-like self to Your self. I praise You in worship.

70. The Universal Lord!

The Five elements, such as the Water, Earth, Fire, Wind and Ether have all originated from You, You are the cause and source of all lives, but You remain with no cause or origin. In You, end all the lives, for You are the end. But Yourself remain Endless. Our five senses cannot perceive You or reach You as You spread out and fill everything because You are so fine, delicate and mysterious. I praise You again.

8. REVELLING IN BLISS

71. I want pure bliss!

You are the Auspicious One who spells good Omen. You are pure enjoyment and You, My Father, looked at me with a grippling look that day, which gave promise that You would unite with me. But that look did not unite me with You. Oh! What is the good of living then? Whether Your look unites or not is of concern. But only give me that Love for You in my heart which will unite me with Your bejewelled Feet.

72. I want the thrill and joy!

My Lord! I do not want the enjoyment of riches or kingdoms. I only want the vision of Your pair of Lotus Feet. There is no other aim or goal in this birth for me, than to reach Your sacred Feet and stay there. Oh! Father, grant that I keep adoring You with hands on head and palms joined, my body transformed and trembling and my eyes streaming down in tears ceaselessly.

73. I want Your True saint's love!

Oh Master! My Lord! You are the partner of Lady Umadevi seated at Your side, with painted eyes. I became a deceitful and cunning person when I immersed in this worldly life and its pleasures, which are nothing but all falsehood. I do not want to be earth-bound, for everything is perishable. You are the Truth and I want for Myself the love with which Your saints reached Your Feet and mixed with Truth in You.

74. I will be born often to worship You!

Oh Lord! remove my intoxication for this mundane life and pleasures which are all falsehood itself. Remove my lies and make me Your own. I want love for Your jewelled Feet. Grant me Your grace, by calling me a dog-like slave to reach You, so that I, Your slave, wear Your Feet upon my head and often cry, praise to You, I want to worship You. Oh King! by being born again and again, for in all my births You will be with me and nothing will happen to me.

75. You, the Sole Truth!

The Earth and the Heaven worship You. The Four Vedas in search of You recited themselves loudly. But not finding You their tones became sad. And since there is no other Truth except You, we worship You crying that we want not to leave you, the partner of the broad-breast Dame, Uma Devi. What is it that You think about, to come and stay and grant us grace.

76. You transcend thought and speech!

It is not possible to reach the utmost limits to which the mind extends in thought; it is not possible for the mouth to speak words about You in praise; for it not fit in the least, because You transcend all thought and speech. Ah, then how can the world hear and know of You, as the five senses cannot see You or understand You. Oh Master do tell us what is the nature of the mind and where it is, so that we may reach Your Foot.

77. Pity Me!

Oh Lord! When will the time come for me to reach You. To my deceitful self, there is no other way or path to reach You, except through You, for You are the True Being who alone can grant liberation. Oh Esan! do have pity on me and safeguard me from all sorrows. There is no better thing in this world for me a sinner than to be united with You.

78. I think of no one else!

Oh Esan! My good Ruler, as far as my knowledge can discern, I foolishly speak that here on this Earth and in the Heaven above there is nothing except You. You are the spotless One who is a true teacher and who made my base self too Your slave. So my mind will not worship nor think of any other God than You, the matchless One.

79. My past sins!

I am stupid wretch who has failed in the past to reach You, I should have by means of thought, word, deed and listening about You, tried to attain You. But my senses are all weak and I have committed the sin of not being united with You. I have still not thrown myself in the fire, nor have I thrown myself down, nor has my heart yet burst to shame for remaining disunited with You. Oh! My Father, I still live cherishing the hope of reaching You soon.

80. Have I real love?

I have a deceitful and cunning heart which is as hard as iron. And You in Your grace have made one such as me Your slave, Your sacred Feet have united me with You and have fed me cane-juice mixed with grace. But, I have parted from You. Though, there is fire beside me I have not yet burnt myself to death. But here I am living on quite well, feeding my body very well; and if I say that I have true love for You, do not my words sound like a juggler's full of tricks.

9. RAPTURE BLISS

81. I, the Seed of Lies!

You have left me here on this earth for fear that the seeds of lie and falsehood should die. But all those whom You love so well have come and reached Your Feet. And I am here sinking in the deepest depths of fear and anxiety. Our own mendicant God of Arur, do speak and tell me what I should do.

82. The worldlings' mockery!

Your devotees counted me as one among Your fold of those who love You. I was smeared and adorned with sacred ashes by the chief of Your devotees. But then, I was mocked by the worldlings as Your slave. I cannot bear this state any longer. I, Your slave, crave only for You and I should however reach Your Holy Feet.

83. Cannot I see You still!

Oh, Our Lord of Shivaloka, am I not Your slave and cannot You make me Your own? All those who were made Your own by You, have reached Your Holy Feet. But I am a wretch who cannot shake myself free of this painful body, and I do not even follow the path which leads to You. Can I not still see the way of seeing You?

84. Alas! I die

You are gorgeous, glorious light, You are both male and female and You also the Ambrosia which is rare. That day I saw You myself, but at that time, I spent my time and energy in useless vain talk, I do not now know how to see You. I do not strive to search for the path to attain You. I am in a state as if dead and gone. My Lord! I am a dog without might and shame. I do not possess any kind of strength to reach You. With what shall I rise up again?

85. I and falsehood left You!

You are the partner of Dame Umadevi who has deer-like eyes. You are the Essence of all the Vedas, unknown to even the sages. You are the Honey and the Nectar. And You are the One who cannot be seen or found out by the mind. Oh King! overlook and forgive all my faults for I did speak harsh words against You; while all Your devotees have reached Shivaloka, whereas I became earth-bound. Together with the falsehood of these mundane pleasures, I walked the path which led me astray, away from You.

86. But Your saints reached You!

I went astray, away from You because Maya—mother of all illusions made me follow the path of falsehood, from which there is no return. Thereby, I have lost true love for You, which I cannot gain hereafter. The saints who wholly sought You, with no other attraction, but by following the supreme path shown by You, and with no other help except Your own, have performed the rarest deeds of virtue and have reached Your Feet, Oh Lord Shiva!

87. I am a blind cow!

My master, I, Your slave, yearn for nothing, but plead

to You to grant me True love for own pair of Feet. I have strayed away from the path of righteousness and liberation, while Your saints have left this world to which there is no return through birth and death cycle, and have reached You. Among the village cows that bellow there is even a blind cow which also bellows along with the others. So too, I, who am without love for Your pair of Feet, weep fondly near Your saints who have great love for You.

88. I followed not Your saints!

While Your saints worshipped You in the manner as wax melting on fire, they were able to at least catch sight of Your glittering Golden Feet and so followed You. But I, a good for nothing in this birth, by which my birth has become a useless one, did not follow their path. I just wept, but with no love for You in my heart. I cannot understand by what means I should henceforth worship You. Oh, Do tell me, Oh, Lord, that I may reach You soon.

89. Powder my sins and save me!

You cure the birth-maladies of those tired and aged saints who bow to You in respect and love and You even bestow Your jewelled Feet upon them. If I have not yet reached that higher state, then it is too good for me, Oh! You, the True One, to shake myself free from my falsehood. I am like a bamboo very stiff and proud. So, powder my sins of stiff pride and make me supple and grant me quickly Your cooling Foot to save me.

90. Could I attain You by crying?

I am a mortal being who is perishable and so all my self is false. So too, my perishable heart is false and the love in it is also false. Despite the fact that I am sinful, if I concentrate on You the Eternal Being and weep, can I not wholly attain You? I become so ecstatic when I come close to You for You are the luscious Lord who is honey, ambrosia and cane-juice. I strongly desire to see You, so make known to me, Your slave, in Your grace, the way to come and attain You.

10. SELF-FORGETTING ECSTASY

91. The true saints and myself!

You, the flood of great mercy which does not change in any way, made Your own true lovers who love You immensely, to come to you, and they received the gift of the state of Oneness with Your Lotus flower-like Feet. Oh! You, the Truthful and endless One came down to earth in simple yet bright human form and looked at me with mercy. At that time itself, I attained You. Before this, I was caught up by Maya and its illusions and in all my births I was just lying in the meanest state like a dog whose breast was unsundered, what fall is this?

92. I know not Your Value!

Oh You! the partner of the maid with good eyes painted bright, since the time when You came to make me Your own, I did not, at that time, know Your worth and value. Just as a child does not know the value or worth of a golden cup held in its palms so too, I did not consider You as a rare one, You are my bright one who is adorned with sacred ashes. Your lovers who are the saints and sages have attained Your own pure essence. After taking hold of me, You have left me to fall into this world of illusions and live in falsehood. How can You leave me here and You go away? Does this action of Yours ever become you?

93. Could I be left like this?

I am not worthy to receive You, Oh! You, who have Feet like Lotus flower. I have no fitness of any kind but of falsehood I am full. Though You gave me Your gracious look and asked me to come to You, I took no pains or efforts to reach You, and I have filled my heart full with deceit and cunning, for I thought very greatly of this worldly life, which is not permanent. But You of crimson form were united with all Your loving saints who received Your grace. Is it just that You should have placed me here in this transient world; my Lord is there no end to the sins of my own wasteful self?

94. Your great miracle!

You are the partner of the maid with good and fragrant locks of hair. You made me love Your Feet. By Your magic Feat, You created a soft and ripe fruit out of stone. Oh, You, the spotless mystic Ether. You are my Lord, can You not redeem me? Whatever be my means and whatever be my deeds Your mercy knows no limit and so, why not You disclose Your own pair of jewelled Feet to me, as there is no love in me for Your own pair of anklet Feet.

95. You made me dance!

You are the One whom the heavenly ones themselves cannot understand or know at all. You are the one whom the Vedas find it difficult to expound. You are One whom all the rest of the worlds cannot even catch glimpse of. You have sweetly made me Your own, so that I may know You. You have caused this fleshy body of mine to dance in every birth. You had melted Yourself and made me drink of You. You had caused my soul to move in rhythmic, mystic dance. Had You not done all these for my bonds to this worldly life to die?

96. Though vile, I am Yours!

It is only You who can reap a harvest without seeds being sown. The whole of Heaven, the whole of Earth and all the rest of things can be created by You without even sowing a seed. It is only You who sustains and also conceals everything. I was a cheat for I had attached myself to the world and You instead charged my low and deceitful self with great frenzy. You had also placed me by the side of Your own Temple gates. You had made me a servant of Your great saints. And You are my owner. A man would not chop off a tree which was once planted by him even though it proves to be rotten, like that, I have been created by You and so, You, my master do not overlook me.

97. I praise!

I praise You, my Lord and Owner. Hereafter, I have no other support except You. You are the greatest Lord of all the Heavenly Ones and so I praise You, I praise You the One who has called me to serve You. Before You, I have become the meanest one of all. I praise You for You are my Lord of endless, Infinite mercy. I praise you for You are the First and You are the End of everything. I offer You my praise.

98. Pity my poor self!

You are my Father, my divine Ambrosia. You are the Supreme bliss. You are the sweetest honey that rushes into, and fills my heart full while my heart melts for You. You made me a privileged person by making me a kinsman of Your own favourite saints. You became the life-giving Food for me to taste and drink. You are the One who wears the brightest crown and You are my help on whom I can depend firmly. Oh King, You are a treasure in need for Your saints. Is it just for You to have placed me in this deceitful world to sorrow, pine away and die? Do speak my Lord.

99. Bid me come to You!

You are our King, our Lord. Just command me to come to You. You are the source for Vishnu and Brahman, the four-faced one and for the rest that is found here. You invite me to come to You do accept me. You are the Lord who outlasts the complete end of all at the time of destruction. Do invite me to come to You, Oh Lord! Call me that I come with love in my heart for Your bejewelled Feet. Oh! You, who wipes away the sins of one and all who come to You. Command me to come to You so that my tongue must sing Your glories and chant Your praises.

100. My Earnest Prayer!

I praise You for I long to sing to You alone. I long also to sing and praise You with my body melting in Ecstasy. My dog-like self would like to blend itself and stay at Your flower-like jewelled Feet, which dance in mystic Ether. I praise You and pray to You to rid me of this body which is a shell of worms inside. I earnestly long that all my falsehood drop away from me. You are the Truthful One to Your saints, I earnestly pray to show mercy and grant me too the truest salvation. I offer You my praises and adoration.

6. Neethal Vinnappam (Forsake Me Not)

1. Hold me up!

You, the Lord riding on a bull as Your chariot, You who put on the tiger's skin and You, Oh! Lord with braided locks, the King of lasting Uttharakosamangai made me, a mean and low person who was wallowing in the worldly pleasures, Your slave by Your grace. Do not forsake me, for I am sinking into this mundane life again. So, support and hold me up again.

2. I, a Deserter!

Oh! You, the King of Uttharakosamangai do not forsake me, as I have not yet given up my lustful nature of admiring the red lips of the broad-breast maids. I have become a deserter and have gone away from You because I have given up myself to lust. In spite of knowing my nature so well You have still made me Yours. What is the reason for this? I too have undertaken to serve You in a small way. So, I am within the fold of Your saints. And I plead to You not to leave me here in this world.

3. You Rearest Me!

The trees by the river banks have found the roots deep

into the soil. However strong they are, they fall due to soil erosion. Likewise, my five senses are deeply rooted in lust and they are eroded by my lustful activities. Oh! You, of bright Arur do not forsake me. You, the King of Uttharakosamangai, do not let me perish. You whose half consists of the Lady Umadevi should bring me back to the right path and look after me.

4. I slipped from You!

With growing grace, You had taken my hands into Your own and held me tight. But even then I slipped away from Your hold and have gone after worldly activities in which I have succeeded and shine still, in spite of knowing their falsehood. You, the King of Holy Uttharakosamangai, have a tender white moon on Your long braids which shines. You are the Lightning light of Golden form. So, I plead to You not to forsake me.

5. I declined Your proffered Nectar!

You are the Lord who wears fragrant flowers on Your braids ploughed by the sweet-mouthed bees. You, the King of Holy Uttharakosamangai, met me and spontaneously offered me and fed me with Your gracious nectar which I declined. And just like a moth which is always attracted to a bright flame of light, I, too, for a long time have fallen a prey to the sweet and tender words of the maidens. Yet do not desert me.

6. Forgive my faults!

Oh! My Gem! When You gave me Your good grace, I refused to accept it. So do not forsake me in hatred, but destroy my bunch of evil sins and make me Your own. Oh King of Holy Uttharakosamangai, I pray You to forgive all

the faults of a petty dog like me, because all great Ones forgive
the faults of the small ones.

7. You cure birth maladies!

King of lasting Uttharakosamangai! forsake me not. Oh!
Shiva of crimson form Your throat is dark with poison that
You had drunk. You are the one who cured my humble self
of all my birth-maladies and You also thought me who is
false, worthy of Your grace and so You made me Yours.

8. I am pulled on either side!

Perspiringly I keep wondering what way Your glorious
grace is going to adopt to cure all my faults. You, the King
of Holy Uttharakosamangai, whose flower-wreathed bull
frightened the enemies with its tremendous bellows. So do
not forsake me; for my five senses and fear pull my sinful
self in both ways—the good and the bad.

9. I pined with dishevelled locks!

I parted from You and pined and cried with dishevelled
hair, like an ant which is within a firebrand lighted at both
ends, struggling to come out. Oh! do not give up, You, the
Lord of the three great worlds. You, the King of everlasting
Uttharakosamangai, You have the war Trident which shines
in Your Hands.

10. I wear away!

Though I have reached Your glittering Feet, yet my body
wears away and I have become weak. Do not forsake me.
Oh! You, the King of Holy Uttharakosamangai, Your fine
gardens and groves resound with the humming and songs of
bees. And You burnt the cities of Your enemies with a big
and mighty bow.

11. I am estranged from You!

My five senses have been cunning that they have cheated me so well and that is why I have separated myself from Your jewelled Flower Feet. Even then do not forsake me. You are the honey that springs in my sinful self. Oh! Eternal and noble King of Uttharakosamangai, Your golden form which is adorned with ashes shines brilliantly.

12. I am deceived by my five senses!

Although Your noble self has made me Your own, I have parted from You because my own five senses have deceived me. But do not forsake me. You are the King of lasting Uttharakosamangai whose spear would kill Your dreadful enemies. You are the Ambrosia which is like a great Sea of clear drink to even my cruel self, who is allowed to taste of it.

13. I lap water even in a Sea!

You are the One who has made the bodies of Your saints a temple for You to dwell therein. You are the nectar found in the flower. Oh Gem, You are the Ambrosia, the luxurious drink of the Gods. You are my own flood of honey. Just as a dog laps water in the vast Sea, Your mercy which is like a Sea has not been heartily tasted by me. Even then, Oh King of Uttharakosamangai, do not give me up.

14. Thirst amidst Water!

Just as a person stands with a parched tongue when even in the middle of a flood, I too stand unable to free myself from my numerous sorrows, even though I have Your grace. In spite of this, do not desert me. Oh King of Uttharakosamangai, You dwell in the hearts of the saints who love You. In Your Grace, fill my cunning self with such joy that none has ever experienced and known yet.

15. I have not reached You!

Oh! King of Uttharakosamangai, Your beautiful Feet which are the source of Brightness, shine brighter than all the truest lights. Although I saw Your jewelled Feet, with great joy in my heart, I was not ready to come out of the worldly pleasures for You to mix me in Grace, because I was still fettered and earth-bound. You are my loving master, Lord and Father who rules me. So do not think of ever deserting me.

16. None to tell me, fear not!

You are matchless, unparalleled and there is none other like You, in truth You are alone. King of lasting Uttharakosamangai, You are like lightning. I have been wandering about away from You and have become very tired as there has been no one to call me son and tell me not to fear. Oh, My rarest wealth, You are a Mother to me and a Father to me. So, do not renounce me.

17. You are my only refuge!

You are the Truth, You are the Grace, You are the drink of Your true saints. You, the King of Uttharakosamangai, are the fruit of knowledge. You dispel the darkness of ignorance and bring the light of wisdom. You are this world and the next too. You are a fear to those who scorn Your fame. Do not give me up as You are the only refuge for my lonely self.

18. Sell or pledge me!

Oh! King of lasting Uttharakosamangai, You drank poison as one could drink ambrosia. You are the Balm which heals the curves of all those who are caused to suffer by the birth, disease. Do make me Your own, govern me, sell me or even pledge me. I am Your latest slave, so do not forsake me.

19. Set fire to my sins!

You killed the hill-like elephant, thereby frightening Your dainty spouse. My sins are as fierce as a jungle. Set fire of Your abiding grace to all my sins so as to burn and destroy them all, King of Uttharakosamangai, govern me by uprooting all my births. You are the most handsome one, and do not ever forsake me.

20. I a tendril without a prop!

Oh! You are the tender One, dwell above and beyond the reach of Gods. Oh! King of Uttharakosamangai, You are the five elements such as the Ether, the Fire, the Water, the Earth and the Wind. I am like a creeper's tendril which cannot find any support to wind itself and grow and so, I am pained very much. My only cry is that You should not give up my own rotting self.

21. I am crushed by my senses!

Just as an elephant, in its wildest fight, crushes the tiny grass and shrubs, so too, I am tossed about and crushed by my five senses. Oh! You, the luminous one, I want You to be the honey, milk, sweet sugarcane juice and nectar in my sinful heart and melt my flesh and bones and make me Yours. Oh! My master, do not renounce me.

22. You are near to friends!

Oh! the glittering one, You are the white one because of the shining splendour of the sacred ash with which You have adorned Yourself. You are very near to the hearts of Your truest saints. But You are very far away to the others for whom it is very difficult to even know You. You are feminine, ancient masculine and an eunuch too. Do not forsake me as unworthy of You.

23. I shrink in love!

I have been given this human birth but I have just multiplied my sins and I have shrunk in my love for You. I am Your worthless slave, do not forsake me, if You leave me away then I will perish and there will be no one except You to hold me up because You are the very source of my own life. You dwell in me as the very basis of my life and I have gained wisdom through the sufferings in my life.

24. I am a flame of white heat!

You wear the skin of a strong-trunked elephant as a robe. I am a flame of white heat and I pride myself with false beliefs and useless empty talks. I give up all that is good and my tendency is to do evil. I am like ants in a jar of ghee; my senses prey upon me thus preventing me from joining and merging with You. I pray that such a thing should not happen to me, so do not forsake me.

25. I am a worm amidst ants!

I am eaten by my five senses and so I lie like a tender worm which lies in the midst of ants which keep growing at it. You are the state called bliss and so You are far too higher than the heavens for those who know Your fragrant Feet which crushed and killed the God of death, You are the Great One who does depart from Your saints. So too, I pray do not give me up, a vain and lonely person.

26. I am fish, out of water!

The white crescent moon floats like a boat on the rising tides of the Ganges river which lives on Your own braids of hair. From the time I parted from You, I am like a tiny fish in a dried up stream. Oh! You the Heavenly priceless Gem, do not ever forsake me. Now, I wither and faint in utter fear.

27. I am victim to passion!

I was so attracted by the maids with white teeth resembling pearls and I reached their hill-like breasts, and then I shrank and fell into a world of passions and became its victim. You are the Gem who has cleaned me of all my impurities and has placed me in the company of Your saints whose bodies tremble in awe and love, and in Your mercy, You made me Your own. I beg You, do not desert me but show me Your celestial Feet once more.

28. I went the wrong path!

I was torched and cheated by my five senses. I was so distracted that I strayed along the path of wrongful deeds and became grief-stricken. While heaven and earth shook in despair, You, in Your mercy, ate the poison from the Sea. Oh! You are the master and the Lord worthy of worship. I, Your slave, shiver in grief and fear. So, do not forsake me.

29. I am freed from caste!

You made me free from the bonds like caste and all other Faults. You are the matchless. My Father and my Master with lotus form that is lovely and bedecked with cassia garland which is bright like the Gold. You made the mountain as Your bow of Victory. Like curd, which is churned by the churning rod, I am churned by the five-fold bonds of the senses. Do not give me up!

30. I am the seed of woes!

You wear a garland of white skulls and on Your body, You adorn Yourself with bunches of cassia made into wreaths and around Your neck wear the entrails as long as a garland.

You are the pure essence. You smear Yourself with red sandalpaste and white ashes. I am burnt up by my five senses which are aflame like the curd which is churned by the churning stick. In this birth, I am the seed of sorrows. So, save me and do not forsake me.

31. Your prowess!

Oh! You wondrous one, You are pure essence. You are the cool water, the sky, the wind, the earth and the fire. You are of different hues such as black, white and green. The colour of Your form is red. You adorn Yourself with a bright-hooded snake for Your sash, You have conquered the war-ring, rough elephant of broad wide feet too. Do not forsake me, I pray!

32. I am a victim to senses!

Your throat is black since You put Yourself to the test of drinking rare poison that sprang from the Sea. Oh! Grand and glittering Gem, none but Your saints alone can touch and feel Your Holy self. I am struck by my fearful senses and have become a victim to them. It is too difficult for me to leave You and I cannot bear it. So, do not desert me.

33. I am drunk with mercy-wine!

I followed the path of my own wishes. Oh Master! root out my shrub of worldly lusts which hinders me. Now I am drunk with wine of Your mercy and so I am filled with joy and blabber. Do not give me up, but grant me as of old Your fragrant Feet and make me Yours and command me to serve You well.

34. I was self-willed!

You are the Supreme Lord of Kailash, do speak to me,

for I, by living here on this earth, am empty without joy in my heart. It is because I did everything according to my own will and pleasure. But now I hurry to do Your will alone. When will You like the plantain fruit mellow my heart, and reach me to be the sweet and scented honey for me to taste. Do not renounce me.

35. Even me, You loved!

You are the Lord of Lords! You are Haran. You love Your saints whose love has been tested by You. You love even me who is false. You, without any differentiation, adorn Yourself with both the snake and the hare-like moon alike. Oh! My Lord, do not desert me, for this birth of mine has come in the form of a five-mouthed snake which fights and frightens me. It drives my sinful self locked in fear to seek shelter in caves thus disabling me to see You.

36. I am burnt by my senses!

You are the Heaven's strong King. Your bright braid is adorned with Mandara flowers with sweet Nectar. That is why the bees that learn the loud-key tunes softly hum around this sweet nectar. While the bees are able to throng Your honey dipped plait, I am unable to do so because like fire that burns with smoke amidst the cluster of trees, I am burnt by my five senses which are in turn burnt by fire. Will You not save me who is burnt by my own passions?

37. Cheer me up!

Your spouse is Umadevi, the maid of billows with white teeth and black-painted eyes. You are Bunangan of the Golden Feet with form the colour of God. My mighty bad deeds clustering and mounting like hills do jeer at me as do the clustering hills. My ignorant self, which is without knowledge, will not live unless You, my King, tell me not to have fear about the faults committed by me. Will You not clear me up?

38. I parted from You!

You are the King of the burning ghat. You are the light of pure consciousness that pervades everywhere. You are the flame that leaps and burns. You are the Ambrosia for Your saints, without practices, no one can attain You. I have no other support or help for You are my sole help that kills my loneliness. I parted from You because I have become a prey to my senses which trouble me. I am caught up in my lustful passions and I am unable to come out of it. Will You not save me?

39. I was swollen-headed!

While You were the only help which was present then, I did not take notice of You, for my head was swollen with pride as I walked headlong with evil sins as my only friend. Now too, You are the sole help to my sinful mind. You are the life and source of my own life, You are my unfailing treasure. Do not forsake me, I cannot any longer endure my painful and oppressive body to be caught up in the repulsive net of lust.

40. I was sensuous!

You are the one who wears the white moon's most slender crescent, You are the home of mercy, the chief of Mount Kailash, the spouse of Umadevi, the Mountain maid and You are the source of my life too. I have been caught up in a net, as it were, by the looks of those maids whose eyes are like the eyes and looks of the deer caught up in a net. Since then I have been roaming about and grieving all the time. Will You not come to my rescue?

41. I was bitten by crocodiles!

My goal is to attain bliss, and You, Shiva are my goal of bliss. You are the spouse of Umadevi whose breasts are adorned and bedecked. Completely and violently, I immersed myself within the hottest flood of lust and felt deep sorrow, because I was bitten by crocodiles, that is, the red-lipped maids. I cannot any more endure to carry this foul-smelling, fleshy body which brings only sorrows. Is it just for You to leave me in this state? Oh! do not forsake me.

42. I do not give up this flesh of mine!

Oh King! You make the moon and the snake dwell on You. When the bright snake living within the white skull raised, spread and closed its hood, the moon seeing this hid itself in the water which flows from Your braid as the Ganges River. Though You, in Your mercy, gave me, Your slave, Your Feet as my refuge, I rejected it as I was ill-fated, not able to forget and shuffle off my fleshy body. Oh Lord! When You can house these two contrasting things, the moon and the snake, why not You give me wisdom? Oh! protect me!

43. I knew not how to mix with love!

You are the one who uttered and expounded the mystic and the highest truth. You are beyond the explanation and description of all words. You are the first of the living band of saints. You are everything and even the lust. Oh King! I am ignorant of the way of blending and merging with You. You are the blissful light to me a little one. So, do not give me up!

44. I was melted by lust!

I melted like butter in the fiercest flame of lust of maidens whose eyes are like sharp darts. Do not forsake me, my

Lord! but place me in the midst of the company of Your band of saints who worship before Your grand fragrant flower Feet. My Master! I worship You, do not give me up as one who commits faults, I will sing Your praises.

45. I stand distressed!

I have neither sung Your praise nor have I even worshipped You with bowed head. When You, the Gem parted from me and concealed Yourself, I did not bother to cast off this fleshy body of mine for Your sake, but went after lustful pleasures. After Your departure, I never cried with amazement and never cared to question: Oh, where is Shiva? Who has seen him? Neither did I run helter-skelter in search of You, looking for You; neither did I fall, nor did my heart melt for You. I just stood in vain, distressed.

46. I am a fly on jack-fruit!

Just as flies hover about and then sit upon the sweet jack-fruits, I too was lusting about for the breasts of the fawn-eyed maidens. Because of this, will You renounce me? If You forsake me then, I will reproach You and call You the "Black cloud-throated one" who ate the poison of the Sea. Also, I will chide You as the unqualified one without knowledge and wisdom. Again, I will say You are the 'Waning Moon'— a man without character and good qualities. I will also say that You are just an ordinary human being as any one of us. I will call You as an 'Old Lord'.

47. I was left blinking!

Pearls and conch are carried and brought along with the rolling waters of the Ganges River. There are fragrant flowers that float upon the waters. Your braids like a dam keep the waters bound. Upon these waters, like a boat, swims the crescent moon which You wear as Your wreath. And I reached Your flawless, ancient band of saints who worship and serve at Your Feet. But then, I withdrew and fell back. I became so inferior and kept blinking and reviled at You. Will You not take notice of me?

48. I shall trumpet You as my Lord!

You wear wreaths made of star-like skulls upon Your crown. You bedeck Yourself with fire-like snake jewels. So, You are the hero. You who are so, do not leave me in a dreadful state. If I am placed in such a base state, when questioned by noble men "Whose slave are you?" then, I will tell them that 'I am the slave of all great saints/slaves of the King of Uttharakosamangai' and Your state will become sorry and they will laugh.

49. I shall revile at You!

If You hate me and forsake me saying that I am a wrong-doer and commit faults, then, I will proclaim that Your action is incorrect and have all the noble men laugh at my cursed life. And then through all my actions, I will reveal that I am Your slave. Even then, will You separate me and push me aside from You? If You do such a thing, then, I shall swear at You and call You "The Tusker-hide mad, the tiger-skin mad, the poison food mad, the burning-ghat mad and the man as One who owns me as His slave."

50. Your immense sacrifice!

Whether I revile at You or praise You, I melt at my own faults and repent feeling very sorry for my actions. So, do not forsake me. You are the One who can make me Your own as I am Your slave. You are the bright red coral mount. Fill me with wisdom too. You are privileged to consume sweet nectar. But You ate fiery poison for the sake of the petty souls, so that they might live. This reveals Your great sacrifice. So too, remove my ignorance and give me wisdom.

7. Thiruvembavai (Morning Bath of Maidens)

1. She responds not to our songs!

As we walked along the streets, we sang about the Rare One, who is splendorous and great and who knows no beginning or end. Oh! Maid with large and shining eyes, why did You sleep on, though You had heard our songs. Were Your ears so hard and dull? Such things as fitful sobbing, self-forgetting in ecstasy, rolling down from the flowery bed should have happened when the resounding praises of the Great God's jewelled Feet chanted by us were heard. You did not wake up. All You did was, slept on and on. Why had this happened? Is this Your nature, my friend, Embavai?

2. She is delighted with her couch!

When we used to talk of Him all night and day, You jewelled maid used to say that all Your love was for Him who is the Supreme Light. Then, when did You become enamoured and bound to this flowery couch? Oh! You, maids bedecked with jewels, are all these of little value or importance to You? This is not the time and place to talk or act lightly and tease in a playful way. Even the heavenly ones who are so knowledgeable feel that they are unworthy to praise Him and so hesitate and fall back. Such a one who is Shivaloka's Bright One and Esan of Thillai's Chittrambalam, comes in grace to grant mercy. His flowery Feet for us to worship, we who have no knowledge of Him, but just a little love for Him, are we worthy to sing praises about Him? Oh! Embavai!

3. Her love is no hoax!

Oh You! maiden with pearl-like white teeth, You used to rise early in those days, come in front and with surging love speak very sweetly of Him saying that He is Your Father, Your blissful One and Your ambrosia. But now, such a one as You, why do You sleep still. Wake up and come and unlatch the door of Your house. Is Your love just a pretence then? You are Esan's old and loving saints who are privileged too. But we are beginners who have just become His slaves. There is no harm if You will come to drive away the meanness from us. We very well know of Your love for Him? Will not You the pure-minded and good sing of our Lord Shiva? Don't we also deserve to sing of Him Oh! Embavai.

4. We cannot count, count Yourself!

You, maid of glittering pearl-like teeth, has it not yet dawned for You? Have all the maids who speak words sweetly like pretty parrots, arrived, asks the sleeping maid. The one who has arrived says that they would count and tell her the exact number. She further tells her not to sleep with closed eyes and waste her time by sleeping. Instead, she goes on to say that they should sing of Him who is matchless among even the Heavenly Ones, who is the sweet Ambrosia and the One whom the Vedas praise as their Highest Essence. The One who was sleeping continued to sleep, unmindful of the words spoken by those who had come. Therefore, they emphatically told her to count the arrivals, for they were wasting their time in counting and if they were a few then she could continue her sleep, Oh! Embavai.

5. She had feigned her love!

Shiva, the Mighty Mount cannot be known or seen by even the Gods Mal and the four-faced Brahman. How can we earthly maidens know and see Him? We speak in falsehood when we say we can know Him and see Him. Your mouths surge with milk and honey when you talk so sweetly. Oh! Maid of guileful mind, come and open your door. The earth and heavens and all the rest do not know Him and about Him. So, we can sing His beautiful form as far as our knowledge goes. We can also sing of His greatness in making us His own and fondling us in grace. Yet, you will not wake up and you will not see when we cry aloud "Oh Shiva, Oh Shiva". You of perfumed locks, is this your nature to sleep thus? Oh! Embavai.

6. She has forgotten her promise!

The Fawn-like maid herself had the previous day promised the others that she would come the next day and wake them all up. Now, the maids who have come to wake her up ask whether her promise has gone with the wind. They say it's shame to be still asleep and ask whether it has yet dawned for her? The Heavens, the Earth and all the worlds are unable to know Him. But, He voluntarily comes and shows His best mercy and makes us His with grace. We have come to sing about His lofty Feet. So, get up and unlatch your door for us to come. Will not your body melt? Will you not sing? The King who rules us all and all the rest as His? Does this suit you? Oh! Embavai.

7. She has forgotten her old ways of love!

Oh! Mother, are there such trifling traits in you? It is very difficult and hard for many to think on Him and of Him. Only the heavenly ones know that He is the only one and He is of mighty glory. In the past, when you used to hear His signal organs' sounds, you used to open your mouth and cry 'Oh Shiva'. Even before the name of Tennavan was uttered, you used to melt like wax on fire. And in your presence, each of us used to sing of Him as 'My Lord', 'Sweet Ambrosia' and so on. Are you the one who listened to us before, now still asleep and lolling like the fools whose hearts are very hard without feelings? How funny is this sleep? Oh! Embavai.

8. It has dawned, rise and open the door!

While the cocks crow, while the birds twitter on every side producing sweet music and while the conches blow on every side, we sing about that peerless light who is Supreme, who is that peerless great mercy and that peerless essence who is above everything. When we sang about Him, did you not hear our song? Oh! Blessings to you. But what king of sleep is this which prevents you from opening the door. Is this the way of loving Shiva whose commands run everywhere? Come, let us sing of Him, who stands as the Foremost One when every age is destroyed and who is the partner of Umadevi. Oh! Embavai.

9. Joint petition to Shiva!

You, ancient Being, You are older than the most ancient beings. Yet, You of latest novelty are quite later than the latest. We, Your lucky slaves, have been blessed to have You as our Lord. We would bow at the Feet of Your devotees whom You love and be their own by right. They alone shall be our true husbands. And whatever they command in joy, for us to do, we shall render service to them as their slaves. If only You bestow this one boon on us, our Lord, then we will have nothing at all to grieve. Oh! Embavai.

10. Queries to temple maids!

His Flowery Feet which are beyond the description of words, rest beneath the seven deep worlds which have no boundary. His crown which is adorned with a fragrant flower-wreath is the crowning end of all. Umadevi is His one half and so He is said to have not one form alone. Even if the Vedas, the Heaven and the earth praise Him, His praise grows endlessly because they cannot praise Him sufficiently. He is a unique friend who cannot be explained by words. He lives in the hearts of His devotees. The maids who dwell in Shiva's shrines are of the purest stock. He does not have a place; He does not have a name; He does not have kinsmen or even foes. What then is the manner of singing Him entirely? Oh! Embavai.

11. They dive in temple tank!

Entering the broad and bee-filled tank, we dive and splash and splash the water with our hands and sing of His jewelled Feet. We, Your true slaves, who are direct descendants from You are truly blessed. Oh! Striking and unusual Master, Your form is bright, Your form shines like red-fire. You smear Yourself with white ashes. You are the noble one who is the bridegroom of Umadevi with wide and painted eyes. Oh! Father, we have quite lived out in the manner, all the courses of lives, lived by Your good saints whom You in loving sport have made Your own. Guard us, for fear we become weary in future. Oh! Embavai.

12. They bathe!

He is the only Holy water in which we sing and bathe. We sing and bathe in the water, which is He, so that all our sins and sorrows which bind us in all births might run away from us. You dance with fire in Your hand within the sacred court of Good Thillai. You sport for fun and amusement. You sport by guarding, making and hiding heaven and earth and everything else. They all wish to sing His praises with bangles tinkling, girdles around the waist jingling and sarees making a rustling and bristling noise. With the humming of the beetles on the fair tresses, they plunge into the pond of flowers and praise the Golden Feet of their own Lord. Oh! Embavai, do bathe in the water of that deepest fountain.

13. The vision of Shiva-Sakthi in the tank!

The swelling tank is filled with fresh and blue kuvalai flowers and with rosy lotus buds; the little water-birds of the same family make twittering sounds and snakes inter-lock themselves. And the sins of those who enter the tank, are washed away, this beautiful waterscape has the vision of Shiva-Sakthi in the tank. The maids all decide to get within this tank and plunge and plunge deeply into it, with bangles made of shell tinkling and with anklets clashing, making jingling noise. While, the water along with their breasts which heave with joy also heaves. Oh! Embavai, let us all plunge and bathe in the Lotus-filled water which is fine.

14. They sing the glory of Shiva!

The ecstasy of the maidens while singing is seen in the swinging of the ear-drops and the waving of the golden jewels. Their locks full of wreaths float while the swarms of humming bees play on. They plunge and bathe in the cool water and sing songs on the sacred court of Thillai. The Vedas are not able to sing about His true essence. But the maids sing His essence as just as He is. They sing the glory of that Light and sing about the cassia wreaths that He wears. They sing the glories of Him who is the First One and they sing also of how He becomes the End of everything, but Himself without End. Oh! Embavai, let us sing too of the glorious

Feet of Her who separates us and who brings up all of us with love and special care.

15. The Supreme infatuated God-Mania of Mind!

Now and then, she cries "My Lord", "My Lord" and thus her mouth does not stop with great rapture and to sing of the glories of our Lord. Her pair of eyes do not stop to shed an endless stream of tears. She prostrates now and then but will not bow down her head to the heavenly ones. Oh! Maids, whose breasts are decked with jewels, let us sing with mouth-ful of words of the way this one became quite infatuated for that Mighty King. We will sing also the fact of that true One making her His own. Oh! Embavai, let us plunge and bathe within the flood filled with flowers.

16. The cloud and Parasakthi!

Oh Cloud! You drank the water from the Sea and rose up shining like our Queen Umadevi. You glittered like Her lightning waist. You thundered like the golden anklets on Her Feet. You cast and spread out the rainbow like our Lady's own eyebrow. She is our mistress, who does not part from our King. At the very first thought, with such spontaneous love, She poured Her sweetest grace upon all His living saints in our presence. We too are Your maids, just as You poured love on Your saints do pour Your love, like a rainy cloud, on us who are Your maids.

17. Shiva's visits to our humble abodes!

Such bliss, that is not enjoyed by Vishnu of blood-red eyes, by Brahman of four-fold face, the heavenly ones and all the rest, has now become our own because Shiva has come in the form of a knight who fondled us by His graceful visit to every one of our homes here. He has granted us His golden, red lotus Feet. Oh maid, with dark and fragrant locks, let us for our own good and benefit, plunge into the lotus flood and sing of that prince of beautiful eyes, who is that Rare Nectar to us His slaves, Oh! Embavai.

18. Glory of the Lord of Annamalai!

The shining brightness of the gems studded on the crowns of the heavenly ones fades, when they bow down to worship the Feet of Lord Annamalai. The cool stars lose their shining brightness before Him and fly away. Even the splendorous rays of the shining Sun which drives away darkness become dull as He who is the Nectar, the shining light of heaven, the earth and yet different from these, who is both male and female and the sexless one too, stood before our eyes. Oh! Maid, sing praises of His Holy Feet and plunge and bathe within the pretty flood filled with lotus flowers, Oh! Embavai.

19. The maidens' petition for spiritual partner!

The baby in your hands is your own refuge is the proverb we are afraid to repeat even now. Our Lord! please listen to the prayer we make to You. We want to make only Your saints our husbands. Our breasts should embrace no one except them. Our hands should perform service to no one except You alone. May our eyes by night and day perceive no one and nothing else except You. Our Lord! if You would grant this boon to us just now, then we do not care where the Sun rises at all, Oh! Embavai.

20. The five-fold functions of Lord Shiva!

We praise You, whose flower-like Foot is the first and the beginning of all things. We praise You to grant in loving grace Your tender, rosy Feet which is the end of everything. We praise You, whose golden Feet are the source of all lives. We praise You because Your own pair of Feet is the place of refuge and a source of enjoyment for all lives. We praise You of Lotus Feet, who is not seen by Vishnu and Brahman, we praise You whose Golden Feet saved us, blessed us and made us Your own, in Your loving kindness. We praise You, the one who has blessed us to bathe in the Margazhi (Tamil Calendar's 9th month) flood. Oh! Embavai.

8. Thiruammanai
(Ball Play)

1. The advent of Guru!

Even Vishnu of red eyes and mighty growth, by delving deep into three worlds, was not able to catch the sight of His brightly shining flower-like Feet. Yet, You came down to earth very gracefully and cut away the cycle of our births. You even made men like me who is of low birth, status and rank as Your very own. You are the Lord of the beautiful and sacred town of Perunthurai which is surrounded by coconut groves. You are the one who has eyes of wisdom, His inviting loud call roused and excited me and bestowed His grace on me. Oh Ammanai! Let us sing of His mercy-feet!

2. He charged me with craze!

Those living on earth, the ones in heaven, those living underground and living in other worlds cannot see Shiva though He is present everywhere. He is so great, yet, He can be easily reached by us, because of His grace. He is the Lord of the Southern land and the Sacred town of Perunthurai, who entered into me as rare and sweet Ambrosia and charged me with craze for Him and gave me eternal salvation. Oh Ammanai! Let us sing of Him as the lover who casts His net in the mighty Sea of Love.

3. He came on earth to grace us!

Shiva, leaving Indhra, Vishnu, Brahman and all the rest of the Gods in Heaven, came down to this earth and in His loving mercy, He made men like me of such meanness His very own, His shoulders branded with ash shine brightly. He comes and melts the thoughts and sentiments of His devotees. He is the glorious master of the holy place of Perunthurai, He rode a horse and destroyed all the bonds of attachment. Oh! Ammanai, let us sing the great and endless rapture He has given.

4. Mother like Shiva graced dog-like me!

The heavenly angels, Vishnu, Brahman and Indhra too did penance in the worlds to see Him. They did penance with worn-out bodies and with anthills overgrown around their bodies. And yet, they could not see Him. But with His mother-like self, He came and reached my dog-like self. He graced me best by mixing in my self and thrilling all my pores with joy. His mighty, lustrous, jewelled Foot is all sweet honey and distilled ambrosia, let us sing of it, Oh! Ammanai.

5. He soaked my soul in mercy!

Shiva, the most powerful One of Southern land and One of Holy Perunthurai, made my dog-like, uncultured and meanest self crazy. He kneaded and mellowed my heart and made it ripe as a fruit. He soaked it in His flood of mercy. Like a sage, He killed all my sins and entering Thillai City, He dwells in its sacred Court. Oh! Ammanai, let us sing of that One who rides a raging bull.

6. His pranks with us!

Oh! Maid, have you heard of how that Lord of southern land and Perunthurai of painted walls, has played his pranks with us? He has revealed to us all those things, such as, Shiva, His Lotus Feet and His honey-like mercy too, which He had not shown before. All the while, the worldlings were laughing at us. But He gave us great release and made us all His loving slaves. Oh Ammanai! let us sing of His ways.

7. He dwells in devotee's heart!

Shiva is too far away to those who do not think of Him, but He dwells in the hearts of those who ceaselessly think of Him. He is a knight. He is on the southern land and is One of Perunthurai. He is a saint. His other half is lady Umadevi. He is the Lord who made our dog-like selves as His own servants. He is the True Being who is like a mother to all the seven-fold worlds. He is the One who rules us all. Oh Ammanai! let us sing of Him.

8. He carried earth and got caned!

In His loving grace, He awards a prize for the song that carries music. He is the One who carried in His own form a spouse who is His half. He is the Lord of Perunthurai and Heaven carries His frame. He is the God of the brow which carries the eye. He is the King of the world who earned His wages by carrying earth in noisy Madurai and got beaten by that King on His Golden Form which carries wounds. Oh Ammanai! Let us sing His glory.

9. His ancient ways of gracing!

Shiva owns the crescent moon. He is the owner of the Vedas and the sacred city of Perunthurai too. He wears the three-fold thread and He also rides the big, beautiful bull. He is of various colours, for His heart is black, His form red, and white because He smears His body with white ashes. He is the origin and source of all the worlds. Just like in olden days, He grants unto His ancient saints the great joy which is endless. Oh Ammanai! let us sing of the way in which the world is amazed at it.

10. His cooling pandinad!

Shiva is the sage who is greater than the Gods who rule in heaven. Also, He stands as the grandest of the grand kings who rule the earth. He belongs to cooling Pandinad which cares for and helps the growth and development of sweet Thillai. He is the partner of the maid Umadevi. At the famous Perunthurai, He showed me His visible Feet and made dog-like self His slave. Oh! Ammanai, let us sing of the King who rules in Annamalai.

11. He made pandiland Shivaloka!

Shiva is the Partner of the maid of pretty breasts. He owns the south and Perunthurai city too. He melts the hearts of those who always reach His Feet endlessly, depending on Him loyally. He made the Pandya Kingdom as a Shivaloka. He is the master whose plait is filled with water for He has the Ganges river on His braids. He lives within the hearts of those who reach His rapture-Feet as their own sole refuge. Oh Ammanai! let us sing of Him who is beyond the sight of one and all.

12. He is the self of all!

Oh! Maid of painted eyes! listen, while other Gods— Vishnu, Brahman and Indhra searched for Shiva in their every birth, He, in his loving grace, made me too His very own in this one birth alone and has also prevented my future births. He is manifested in all things which are real and truth is His Eternal Home. He is the Self that manifests as everything and is the self in everything. He is the salvation of all things. Oh Ammanai! let us sing of that True essence who is our Lord Shiva.

13. His palms never meet to salute!

He wears tinkling bangles on the wrists and dangling earrings on ears which dazzle in dark-hued hair floating the honey which multiplies in the flowers worn on the tresses rife with humming bees. He is the Lord of red form who adorns Himself with white ashes, whose palms do not clasp to pray and He is the One who fills up every place. He is true to His loving ones and He is not known and is nothing to the rest. Oh Ammanai! let us sing of that sage who dwells in Ayyaru.

14. His indoctrination of me!

In all my births, I was born as an elephant and as worm, as human and also divine. In all my births, I was born and dead thus and now have become weary. He, Lord Shiva of His own accord, has reached my fleshy melting body and has driven away all my sins with joy. He came like honey, like milk and cane-juice and the sweetest King and placed me within the fold of His own saints in His loving kindness. Let us sing of the beauteous Feet of such a heavenly one, Oh! Ammanai.

15. His punishment of petty gods!

In His loving mercy, He crushed the moon in Dakshan's sacrifice. He broke the shoulders of Indhra and cut away Ecchan's head. He broke and scattered off the teeth of the sailing Sun above. On every side, He drove the Gods of heaven here and there, and was pleased. Oh Ammanai! let us sing of that Pandian and Lord of Perunthurai which is surrounded with groves and flower gardens. Let us sing of His mandara garlands that adorn Him.

16. He graced me with a rare way!

He mingled in me as my flesh, my soul and heart. He was to me honey, Ambrosia and the candy of sweet cane. In His grace, He showed us the way to liberation which is unknown to the heavenly ones themselves. He is the warrior wearing Cassia flowers of sweet nectar. Let us sing of how He stood as wisdom deathless and sacred! Let us sing of Him who is the Lord of all the countless souls, Oh! Ammanai.

17. I crave for His embrace!

I would wear His beautiful cassia garland, wearing it, I would embrace Shiva's muscular shoulders, and thus embracing them I would stand locked up in Him, lost in ecstasy. I would pretend to shrink and pant for His red lips. I would search for Him with melting heart and while searching think of Shiva's Feet alone. I would faint and then smile with joy. Oh Ammanai! let us sing of the Feet of the Dancer who holds fire in His hands.

18. He is double-distilled honey!

Shiva is the bright partner of the Dame Umadevi whose words are as soft as a parrot. He is the wisest One whom Brahman and Vishnu taking different forms went in search of, but could not find nor know about. He is double-distilled honey who came with ease and stayed with mercy in glorious Perunthurai. He bestows rare grace which is rare for thought. He came as light and stayed as shining light within my heart. Oh Ammanai! let us sing of that gracious sage of tenderness.

19. He is the essence of all!

He is the first of all the three Moorthies and He is the self of all beings and things and the end of all things too. He is the One who bears the holy name of Pingnakam. He is the King of Perunthurai. He is of Heaven. He is the partner of Dame Umadevi. He is the One who resides in Southern Aanaikka (Thiruvanaikka) and Pandiland in south. He is like sweet nectar to those who cry 'my love', 'my sire'. Oh Ammanai! let us all sing of that Father.

20. Let us cling to Him to rid of all other clinging!

Strangers cannot know the true nature of the one who is the Lord of Perunthurai. He presides over Perunthurai, and came elegantly riding on a victory horse. He rid His saints of their follies and sins and He acknowledged their virtues, fondled them and made them His own. Let us hold on tightly to the ancient praise of Him who cuts off all bonds that cling to us. Let us hold on tightly to Him so that we may be rid of all these bonds we cling to. Oh! Ammanai, let us sing of that Great Rapture to which we cling.

9. Thirupporchunnam (The Sacred Golden Dust)

1. Appeal to Sakthis!

Hang up wreaths of pearls and flower garlands, place the sprout pots, incense and lamps, And You Sakthi, Somi and the maid of Earth sing songs of praise with Saraswathi. Oh! You, Sithi, Gowri, Parpathi and Ganges come and wave fir fan. Praise the Father who is the King of Ayyaru, To bathe, let us pound perfumed dust of gold.

2. Let all saints join us!

We must pound the perfumed dust of gold for our Lord Shiva who has matted locks and is wearing flowers. Come, you, maids with eyes like sundered young mangoes and coming sing all of you in chorus. Call in all the saints and let no saint stand in wait outside. Let all bow and worship. He is our Lord and Dancer King. He along with His spouse should make us His own. Let us pound the perfumed dust of gold.

3. Plant the Karpaga bough!

Adorn yourself with beautiful white ashes, Then wash and clean the place. Sprinkle pure gold dust and spread out gems. Plant the boughs of Indhra's Karpaga bough every-where. Place beautiful lamps and hold banners overhead.

Do these for Him who is the head of Indhiran, the King of Heaven and Brahman. He is the friend of Vishnu and the Father of Good Velan. He is the spouse of Umai, who made people like us His own. Let us pound the fitting dust of gold.

4. Adorn the pestles and mortars!

Decorate the pestles with wreaths of gold and gems. Decorate the strong mortar with fine silk cloth. Let us praise the saints of purest love and pray that they may live for long. Let us sing of Ekambam's golden shrine at the Kanchi place which is praised by all the lands. Let us stand firm and root out all deeds which bind us. And let us pound the perfumed dust of gold.

5. Let the petty gods follow us!

Both Brahman and Vishnu carry pot-lamps, but we cannot permit Indhra and other gods and the motley crew of heavenly ones to lift and carry pot-lamps before us, except behind us all. Let us sing of Ekambam's old shrine of the bowman who shot three big forts. Oh! You, Maids of smiling red lips, let us pound the dust of gold to bathe our three-eyed master.

6. All the world is not enough as mortar!

Many noblemen gathered, in order to serve Lord Shiva, they came forward to pound perfumed dust of gold for Him. Lifting many pestles, they said that all the world was not enough as mortar. So great was the number of saints who came and mingled and stood, that all the worlds were not enough to contain them, to see and enjoy this beautiful occasion; Shiva for our own God. He made us all His slaves and gave us His flower-feet to wear. Let us sing of that son-in-law of the Holy Mountain. Let us sing in joy, enumerating His greatness and pound perfumed dust of gold.

7. The worldlings and we laugh at each other!

May the bangles and the armlets tinkle! May the band of saints raise up their voice in joy! May the worldlings jeer at us! May we too mockingly jeer at them! Shiva is the partner of the maid whose soft Feet is adorned with jingling jewels. He is the great supreme Lord and King like mount of gold. Let us pound dust of gold to bathe Him.

8. Appeal to all maidens!

Oh you! simple and good maidens of bright and broad eyes, with tinkling bangles and heaving breasts with the brow and shoulders bright with ash, let us speak and speak the praise of Him, our own King. Let us sing and sing the ways in which He showed His Feet which dimmed the beauty of fresh flowers, and made us who are worse than dogs, His slaves within this birth itself. To bathe Him, let us pound dust of gold.

9. World-Mortar and Meru-Pestle!

With all the wide world as the great mortar, we plant the mighty Mount Meru as the pestle and pour into it plenty of the saffron of truth; let us sing and sing the crimson red, sacred Feet of the high Pandian of Perunthurai. Let us pound the perfumed dust of gold to bathe the sage and beautiful Lord of Thillai with the right hand holding the golden pestle.

10. Dance and pound!

While the pearl-adorned breasts do heave and swell, while bees around the locks play and play, while tear-drops flow from the fish-like eyes, while frenzy, and dances with our Lord, while births sway and swing for others and not for saints, while Father with His grace dances and dances, to bathe Him, let us pound perfumed dust of gold.

11. Let us dance with rapture!

Sing with open mouths with teeth whose lustre of pearl spreads and whose pretty coral lips quiver of the ways in which He made us His own. And sing and sing of how we were made to serve and seek that Lord of ours! and seeking Him with rapturous heart get puzzled and consoled. Let us pound the perfumed dust of gold and dance, to bathe the Dancer of the court.

12. He is false to the false and true to the true!

The dark-hued throat of Shiva is Ambrosia to the angels. He is the bright Ruby Dancer. He is the master and the Lord of all masters. He caught us and made us His and showed us His sacred rareness too. He is false to those who are false and true to the truthful ones. You, good maids of flower-like pair of eyes and shoulders bearing golden jewels, let us sing of Him and pound perfumed dust of gold.

13. Relation between Shiva and Sakthi!

Listen, you, maids of lightning waists and rosy lips, of painted eyes and white teeth and soft music words. My rare ambrosia is our own Father and Lord Shiva. He is the husband, son, father and brother too, to the daughter of Himavat. You, good maids with breasts adorned with gold, let us sing the Feet of Him who is my Father, and pound the sacred, perfumed dust of gold.

14. With quivering lips let pound!

You, jewelled maids, with jingling shells and tinkling anklets too, with flowing garlands round the floating trees, with quivering lips of mouths like crimson fruits, sing of Shivalokam. He has clustering braided plaits wherein the snake hisses while the waves of the Ganges roar. Let us with overflowing love and heaving breasts pound for Him the sacred dust of gold.

15. He is undecaying honey!

He is the juice and the essence of the sweet cane of mystical knowledge. He is that Excellence that is too hard to reach and know. He is sweet honey that does not decay. He is the taste of sweetness of fruits. He is the King who enters hearts and who is quite sweet to taste. He is the Dancer who has snapped away the births and has made us His. While pounding perfumed dust of gold, let us sing and praise Him till our tongues get scarred!

16. Let us sing His greatness!

Let us sing of how we too, together with the living saints, can be saved and how we serve His Feet. He would show His rosy flowery Feet which is unseen by the Gods in Heaven, even in their dreams. He has a wealth of courage and bears the victory flag. He is the victorious Hero of Shivapuram, who destroyed the Forts. Let us sing and sing of His names and pound yellow golden perfumed dust!

17. Let us sing His wearing!

Let us sing of the grand and honey jilled Cassia flowers that adorn Him. Let us sing of Shivapuram. Let us sing of the heavenly moon like a babe on His sacred braid. Let us sing of the mighty bull. And let us sing His arms of Axe and of the Trident in His right hand. Let us sing of how He consumed the poison as His food, that day, to save the world and heaven. Let us pound the sacred perfumed dust of gold.

18. Let us sing His prowess!

Let us sing of how He nipped the head of Ayan and

played with it like a ball, and how He broke the Sun's teeth. Let us sing of how He killed and flayed the tusker. Let us sing of how He kicked the Death God with His left leg; let us sing of how He shot at the triple Forts; let us sing of how He made our poor selves His own; let us stand and dance and sing that virtue. Let us pound dust of gold for that Lord.

19. He is our wealth in Chittrambalam!

Let us sing of the round-shaped wreaths of cassia flowers. Let us sing of the phrenzy flower and sing also of the moon. Let us sing of the Southern Thillai, which is of pure souls. Let us sing of Lord Shiva who is our wealth in sacred Chittrambalam. Let us sing of the snake-girdle that He wears around Him. Let us sing of His wristlets and of the snake too, which stands and sports upon the hollow of His palm. We pound sacred dust of gold for that Holy Lord, Esan.

20. He is all the dwandas!

He is the Lord Shiva who is the Vedas and the Sacrifices;
He is falsehood as much as He is the Truth;
He is the Light as well as the dense darkness;
He is the grief as much as He is the joy;
He is the half and He is the whole as well;
He is the bond and the liberation too!
He is the First as well as the Last. To bathe Him, let us pound the sacred dust of gold!

10. Thirukkothumbi
(The Bumble-Bee)

1. He is Unknown!

The flower-borne God Purandharan, the beautiful and the blessed tongue-borne maid and Naranan and all the four Vedas, the horse-borne Light and all the heavenly ones do not know His Bull-borne Feet of rosy colour. Do reach that Feet alone and blow, Oh! Bumble-bee.

2. He made me His!

What would happen at myself, my mind and my own knowledge of the spiritual mysteries too? Nobody would have known me, had not the Lord of Gods made me His own. He, of the Temple Court, begs for food in a mad one's fleshy skull. Let us reach His honey-filled Lotus Feet alone and blow, Oh! Bumble-bee.

3. He is the bliss-honey!

Do not desire to taste with lips the nectar that drops like millet seeds from flowers. He always melts all bones and pours the rapture-honey whenever He is thought of, whenever He is seen and whenever He is spoken of. So, may you reach that dancer alone and blow, Oh! Bumble-bee.

4. His Condescension!

You, my father, have seen a love like that of Kannappan's rich love and You have seen also my poor self which lacks love; yet You have made me too Your own in Your grace and have called me to come to You with great mercy. Go to and reach that bright and white ash-wearer alone and blow, Oh! Bumble-bee.

5. Worship no false Gods!

Indeed, all those Gods are gods. But on earth, they rave and rant thus speak of false gods saying that they alone are gods. But, even though I am void of love, I cling to God Shiva, the God of truthful Gods, to snap off all my bonds. Reach Him alone and blow, Oh! Bumble-bee.

6. He cured me of attachments!

I live within this world filled with delusions like hoarded wealth, women, children, lineage and learning and He, the Lord Shiva has cleared my mind of aberrations and confusions regarding birth and death. Reach that Lord of mystic vision alone and blow, Oh! Bumble-bee.

7. I will never forget Him!

How can I a wretch forget Sankaran who springs in hearts like Ambrosia even though for an instant. We hate the sight of sinful Ganges which hates His deathless Foot. Reach that doubly noble one alone and blow, Oh! Bumble-bee.

8. He honoured me too!

He stemmed as one, and soared and branched out countlessly. He is my Father who fondled me and placed my dog-like self on a palanquin. He is the Father of my own father and mother. Go to that One alone who is of changeless wealth and blow, Oh! Bumble-bee.

9. He drove my illusions!

I went to Him and stayed at His Feet alone which was my refuge. He, of black-hued throat who transcends all the mental powers, made me free of all illusions regarding birth and death. Go to Him that mercy Sea alone and blow, Oh! Bumble-bee.

10. He is Mother-like!

I was scourged by illness and soon started aging, and like a weanling calf was lying here. And for fear that should I with lust enjoy all the canine pleasures, He, the Lord Shiva came like a mother with great mercy and made me His own slave. Reach that lustrous Lord alone and blow, Oh! Bumble-bee.

11. He scorned me not!

The Lord Shiva did not scorn me as a hard cheat having a brutal mind. But He melted my stony heart and made me His with grace. He resides at the Court of beautiful Thillai full of sporting swans. Reach His Pair of Golden Feet alone and blow, Oh! Bumble-bee.

12. He pardoned my faults!

He is the Lord who made my dog-like self sing of His Feet. He is the great One who pardoned all the faults of a friend like me. He does not spurn at me, but He accepts my source in grace. Reach that mother-like Esan alone and blow, Oh! Bumble-bee.

13. The secret of my love!

The fact that I do not have love for Him is known to me

and Him alone. But then, the fact that He has made me His is known to all. He alone is such mercy to make Himself reach me. Go and reach that King and blow pleasantly, Oh! Bumble-bee.

14. He came as Guru!

He is the Germ from whom the earth sprang and yet He is far beyond it too. He came in such grace with Umadevi whose locks were adorned with fragrant flowers. He came on this earth as the formless One and He came again as the Vedic sage and made me His own, too. Go to that Sacred God alone and blow, Oh! Bumble-bee.

15. His mercy saved me!

Had not the Lord of long braid with his spouse Umadevi made me His I would have been very far away from Him and my own mind would have decayed. That Lord Shiva is the heavens, He is all directions and as well as the mighty Sea. Reach His honey-mistling Feet alone and blow, Oh! Bumble-bee.

16. His thought inebriates me!

The moment I thought of His own sacred form which is beyond all thoughts, He came as the Lord of a mighty Flood of mercy and of undeceiving joy. To make my Lord mark me out and to make me His, may you reach that Lord alone and blow, Oh! Bumble-bee.

17. He saved me from false earth!

I lied and was daily immersed in wealth which is fleeting, and I considered it as wealth which is eternal. But then, You made me Your own. You, of Ambalam, are the soul of my own soul, sing of Him as Father, and reach His rosy Feet alone and blow, Oh! Bumble-bee.

18. His ancient form!

The skin of silk, He wears pendants and round ear-rings of the ears. He is adorned with milk-white ash, yellow sandalpaste and green parrot. He wears the trident and the bunch of wristlets. This is His ancient form. See this beauty alone and blow pleasantly, Oh! Bumble-bee.

19. He entered my evil soul!

He did not scorn me as a thief, a cruel one and a vile wretch. That bountiful Lord came and step by step, He dissolved me, and freed me from my mental griefs completely, leaving no trace at all. Reach His jewelled Feet alone and blow, Oh! Bumble-bee.

20. I am proud of being His!

While Brahman and Vishnu stood chagrined because they were despaired of ever approaching Him. He, the Lord Shiva made me proud by placing dog-like me upon a lofty seat and treated me as a worthy one. Please reach the Lord of Fire-Form alone and blow, Oh! Bumble-bee.

11. Thirutthellenam
(A Kind of Maidens' Play)

1. Shiva, our Guru!

Lord Shiva came as a sage and he made us His by show-ing us the form of that sacred Feet which even Vishnu could not see, when He took the form of a boar. He has not a single name, nor has He yet a single form. Let us sing His thousand names and let us beat Thellenam!

2. Let us sing Thiruvaroor!

Lord Shiva of Sacred Perunthurai rooted out all the germs of my birth. Since then, I have known no one else but Him alone. He is the Lord who is formless and who assumes all forms. Let us sing of His holy shrine of Aroor and beat Thellenam!

3. The world laughs at us!

He is that Lord Shiva who stood beyond the knowledge of Hari and Ayan (Brahman), and all the rest of the Gods. Such a One as He, who is Lord, came and melted our hearts and took our service too. When all the world heard about it, it laughed. Let us sing of the ways of Lord Shiva, like these and let us beat Thellenam!

4. We have become Shivam!

Lord Shivam saved us from sinking deep within the worthless fates of all vain gods, and saved us from births and made me His. When that Supreme Jyothi spread its fresh red sheen, we lost ourselves and became Shivam. Let us sing this and beat Thellenam!

5. He entered my soul!

That Shivam whom precious Gods and Vishnu, and Brahman do not know, came in Form, in His grace made us His to the delight of all the world. He burnt the germs of my births by His side-glance and entered me. Let us sing how that bliss came and beat Thellenam!

6. He came on earth!

He is the Lord who wears the sportful snake around His waist. He came on earth with His own maid, Umadevi of Mount Kailash and made us His. Words cannot be found to narrate this, but while speaking this, the inward light glows and flower-like eyes brim with joyful tears. Let us sing this way and beat Thellenam!

7. I have to become God!

Ah! that Shivam who is unknown to Vishnu, Brahman, Indhran and the whole host of Gods, came down to earth and called me and dragged me on His own and made me His own. I became divine the moment the marks of His Flower-Feet were expressed on my head. Let us sing this and beat Thellenam!

8. He made me not to forget Him!

He made me His by driving off my fear of rights and

wrongs and fear of the body of births and deaths, which rotate like a weather-cock. He blessed me so that I should not forget His Feet even by forgetfulness. Let us sing the song of such graces and let us beat Thellenam!

9. He peeled a stone!

Just as though, He would peel a hard stone, He, in His mercy, made me too His own. He is the Lord who made me serve His Golden Feet. Oh! You, maids of lightning waists, red lips and white teeth, let us sing of Him as Thenna, Thenna and beat Thellenam!

10. He entered me while awake!

The gods too even in their dreams cannot see His jewelled Feet. In grace, He entered me with Her of jewelled bamboo-shoulders and caught me while awake and made me His. With loving hearts and sharp and tearful eyes for such of His ways, let us beat Thellenam!

11. All my bondages died!

He mixed in me with a sharp-eyed spouse and made me His! At once, the environment and everything around me died. My bunch of hard sins died also. All illusions on earth died and vain and useless words also died. My acts which were according to my own will too died. Let us sing of these ways and beat Thellenam!

12. He dipped me in love-sea!

While bands of saints roam about and languish for liberation, He blessed an elephant and at the same time, He made myself His own servant. He dipped me and soaked me in the sea of love. Let us sing how that Supreme Light tasted very delicious to us and beat Thellenam!

13. Let us sing His Glory!

He has blessed me in such a unique way and made me His own, so that I do not reach earth, or hell or heaven, or even any other place. It is hard to think of His unique greatness. Let us sing songs of His justice and glory and let us beat Thellenam!

14. He is inaccessible to all knowledge!

Vishnu, Brahman, the sacred scriptures and even the rest of the gods cannot penetrate His secrets. He came in such a subtle form and in pity entered me and melted me. In the thought of this, with tearful eyes, let us beat Thellenam!

15. He is a Sea of mercy!

It is sweet to draw from that wide Sea of Great mercy and then drink with a melting heart, with a swelling frame and a joyous heart. Reaching that, let us think only a Tennan's bright, long Feet, let us, His slaves, sing of our luck and let us beat Thellenam!

16. He is a crazy Lord!

Shiva is ever the novel one. He is the one too whom Indhra, Vishnu and Brahma worship. He is the one who presides in Thillai's sacred court. He is the Lord of Perunthurai and He is the Father who has killed our births. Let us sing how His grace-feet entered our hearts and let us beat Thellenam!

17. He gave us His anklet-feet!

I was lying bewildered in the midst of the great distressful sea of worn-out creeds and inconsistent knowledge of clashing sects. But He drove away my woes and in His grace,

He gave me His pair of sacred feet. Let us praise this act of His and let us beat Thellenam!

18. My 'I' too died!

The five elements, such as the ether, the wind, the fire, the water and the earth should all die. When they die, it is only He who ever remains. He does not die. His nature is that He does not know any weariness. But my flesh, my life, my senses, my mind died in the thought of Him. My egoistic self 'I' died too. Let us sing these ways of His and let us beat Thellenam!

19. He was visible to our eyes!

He is the prime source of all the heavenly ones. He is the seed from whom all those below spring. He is the Ambrosia of the earth and the precious treasure of Vishnu and Brahman. He came and stood and filled our sight. Let us sing of His mercy-feet and crying Thenna, Oh! Thenna, let us beat Thellenam!

20. Let us sing of His dance!

Let us sing of His stock. Let us sing of the crane's quill too that He wears on His head. Let us sing too of the virtue of His maid, Umadevi of conch-bangles. Let us also sing of how He ate the poison, and is the symbol of great sacrifice. Let us sing of that dancer in the court of water-logged Thillai. Let us sing of the play and of His anklets and let us beat Thellenam!

12. Thiruchazhal
(A Dialogue Play
of Damsels)

1. He is the essence of all lives!

What He smears is white ashes and what He wears is the hissing snake. What He speaks is Veda with His sacred mouth. It becomes Him to take to smearing on, speaking and wearing too for He is Esan who is the very essence of every life, Sazhalo!

2. Meaning of His sash etc.

He is my father and my Lord also. He is the Overlord of all. Yet, my dear, why should He wear a patched-up cloth for Kovanam (loin cloth). For His sash, He wears the four Vedas and wears as His own Kovanam the essence of the Eternal Knowledge itself. See Sazhalo!

3. His power!

The burning-ghat, that is the cremation ground, is His own shrine, and His good garment is the tiger's skin. He is without Mother and Father. He is lonely. See my dear! Though He is without mother and father, He is Himself all alone and so is without beginning or end. When He is in great wrath all the worlds will smash completely and become dust. See Sazhalo!

4. His punishment, a grace!

He attacked and inflicted pain and punishment in diverse ways on Brahman, the Formless one! The God of death and the moon. The scars of such wounds would never die! Behold my dear! Oh! You of long locks, is it not an honour for the Gods to be so punished by the great master of the three-fold eye Himself? See Sazhalo!

5. Dakshan's Sacrifice!

Was it fair, my dear, for Him to have chopped off the heads of Dakshan and of Echchan and He to have driven away gang of Gods that flocked the place? Though he drove the gang that flocked, He bestowed His grace on them and He in His grace gave Echchan the head of a mean goat, Sazhalo!

6. Arunachalam!

Shiva, from the deepest world below, stood as a bright flame and rising, soared high above, so that Vishnu who reclines on flower and Brahman could not know and see His Feet. Had he not stood expanding from the deepest world to the sky that day, both Vishnu and Brahman would not have been rid of their arrogance, see Sazhalo!

7. He wears the Ganges!

Hardly had the mountain's daughter, Sakthi, been well placed in Half of His form, when another maid of flood, Ganges, flowed upon His braid. Had not the maid of flood Ganges flowed upon His braided hair, then the danger of all the worlds being washed into the lowest ruinous regions would have occurred, Oh! Sazhalo!

8. Why He ate the poison?

The noisy, deafening roar sprang from within that day, when He swallowed the poison which was rare. What is His skill or feat, my dear? Had He that day not swallowed the poison, then all the heavenly Gods including Vishnu and Brahman, would have perished, see Sazhalo!

9. Why He loves Sakthi?

The Lord who performs the rapture-dance in Southern Thillai's sacred court is a mighty maniac for He takes delight in a Dame. See my dear! Had He not been delighted in a Dame, Oh! mooning, then all men of the wide world would perform penance in heaven and die, see Sazhalo!

10. He soaked me in rapture-flood!

He who Himself has no end has caused the dog-like me too, who had reached Him, to be dipped and soaked within the flood of rapture. See, my dear! The sacred pair of Feet that caused the soaking in the rapture flood are a lofty treasure and wealth to the heavenly Gods, see Sazhalo!

11. Why He wears skeleton wreaths?

Young dame, what is the holy penance of His? He had adorned Himself with bonds and sinews, He is delighted with the skeleton-wreaths on His shoulders. See my dear! Now, listen to the way the skeletons came. When at the end of each age of destruction, the pair had died. Thus He wore their skeletons as His wreaths, see Sazhalo!

12. All Devas, His thralls!

The skin of the forest tiger is His fine garment, the skull is His eating-feasting plate, the burning ghat, that is, the cremation ground is His City. If so, then who would serve Him, my dear? Even if that is so, then you hear this. Both Vishnu and Brahman and the King of the heavens too are His lineal servants, Sazhalo!

13. Why He wedded Umadevi?

Why, my dear, did He before the sacred fire with all the world as witness, wed the Mount-king's daughter who is the great and bright browed Beauty Queen? If He did not wed Umadevi before the fire and had not shown to the world, then all the world would have confused the essence of all arts and knowledge.

14. Why He dances at Thillai?

Why did, my dear, that Lord of the sacred court in Thillai encircled with paddy fields of honey enter there and perform the mystic dance? Had he not thus entered and performed this mystic dance, then all the world would have become good prey for Kali with Her flesh-stained Trident, Sazhalo!

15. Why does He ride a bull?

He is not pleased to mount an elephant, or a horse or a chariot. May I know the reason, my dear, why He is pleased to ride a bull? On that day when He burnt the triple broad forts with fire, the sacred Vishnu form of a mighty bull carried Him, see Sazhalo!

16. He is a Guru and an Avenger!

See my dear, He explained well the mystic meaning of the four Vedas and virtues, beneath a banyan tree to the four people (Janakar, Janandhanar, Janaadhanar and Janadhkumarar) on that day. Though He had explained the virtues that day, from beneath the banyan tree, yet He destroyed all the three, root and branches, see Sazhalo!

17. He is a master mendicant!

He dances in the sacred court of Thillai but roams about begging for His food. My dear, how can such a mendicant be approached as God? This is how this Namban too is deemed as God. The four Vedas do not know Him, but praise Him as Esan and the Lord, see Sazhalo!

18. Why He gave Disc to Mal!

My dear, why did He that day favour and freely give the Good Naranan a disc (Sudarsana Chakra) which is rare and good, with which Naranan chopped off the body of Jalandharan. The Good Naranan had dug out his own eye and offered it as a flower at Haran's Holy Feet, so, He gave the disc to His love.

19. He is unconscious of His greatness!

The spotted skin is His loin cloth and the noisy poison is His rare food. My dear, why did our Lord eat like this? Explain His skill to me. Whatever might our Lord put on and whatever might He eat for food, He does not know His own greatness. That is His nature, see Sazhalo!

20. Why He taught Dharma!

My dear, may I know the reason why He graciously seated under the Banyan tree, taught the rare sages the four-fold theme like virtues? Had He not in His kindness taught the four-fold theme like virtues to the rare sages that day, then they could not have known the world's nature, see Sazhalo!

13. Thiruppoovalli
(Play of Plucking Lilies)

1. His touch and my renunciation!

The moment He placed His sacred pair of Feet upon my head, I renounced everything and was rid of all my helpful kinsmen. He dances in the Sacred Court of Thillai encircled with streams. We sing the glory of that Raft-like God and pluck the lily!

2. He is a honey-comb!

That Lord of Pandiland snapped away my egoistic feelings as my father, my mother and as well as all the rest of the bonds and made me His. Besides, in Idaimaruthura, He is a honey-comb there full of honied rapture. We sing of this and pluck the lily!

3. Let us throw mud into our sin's mouth!

He considered even us as worthy! Our Lord's tenderness to us, who are men and more shameful than dogs, was much greater than a mother's tenderness. He snapped away all delusive births and made us all His own. Let us throw mud in the mouth of our sins which are strong and pluck the lily!

4. The defeat of the rebels!

The ill-famed Dakshan, the Sun, the Moon and Fire all did not worship the Lord of the most famous Thillai town. Therefore, they all got wounds and scars from Veerabhadhra and His vast heavenly hosts. Let us sing how these were caused and pluck lily!

5. He entered my flesh!

Shiva, my Lord, wears honied cassia flowers upon His braid. He came and sought my frame and entered it before the whole world. He also dances while I dance in rapture and cry on. Let us pluck the lily for that Supreme Lord of the Heaven!

6. The four kinds of Triads!

With pity and grace, He granted the Gods the three-fold fire. He strained His scared eyebrows to slash the heads of the three of them. He is that only one who is too hard to know and He assumes the forms of those three. We sing of how that one did burn three forts and pluck the lily!

7. My senses for His service only!

He graced us with heads to bow and worship and mouths with which to praise His Feet. He placed His glorious band of saints here with whom to live and move. My Lord dances with His Dame in the court of pretty Thillai. Let us sing His excellence thus and pluck the lily!

8. He liquidated my deed!

He showed me the gracious path to lead me straight to the goal of the golden feet of the glorious saints and thus He made me His own. Let us praise the greatness of the Lord who wiped off all our old deeds which enslaved us and which sorely distressed us. We sing of this and pluck the lily!

9. He has peeled a stone!

That Great One imprinted His flower Feet upon my body for me to offer worship and perform service to Him. As if He had peeled a stone, that Light of beauty made me His. We sing how His pair of Feet are gold and pluck the lily!

10. He planted His Foot on me!

The Lord of Perunthurai planted His sacred, glorious Feet upon my head so that my mighty lust of the flesh might vanish. Kapali was pleased to eat the dark poison of the Ocean. We sing of the erring Triple Forts and pluck the lily!

11. He is milk and nectar!

The Supreme Lord is milk, He is the Ambrosia and sweet honey all mixed. That Lord thrilled me with His good form and took my heart captive. The way the men praise His tinkling Feet is right. So we sing His praise in that same way and let us pluck the lily!

12. His food was only poison!

He stands as King to the heavenly King Indhra, Vishnu, Brahman and all the rest of the gods. His attributes and signs cannot be known by anyone. Let us sing how the mighty poison springs out of the wide Ocean and how it served as good food for Him to eat, and pluck the lily!

13. He taught under the banyan tree!

He conferred honour on the rare Vedas that day beneath the banyan tree. Then, the heavenly ones and great sages stood well before His perfect jewelled feet and praised Him daily to their hearts' content. Let us sing of the gold dust of

His cassia flowers that He wears and pluck lily!

14. His picture is in my heart!

He stamped the picture of His pair of flower-feet in my heart. Here, He has His dwelling place and lives in Ekambam too. He is that Lord who dances in the court of Thillai surrounded with mighty walls. We sing how that became His Shrine and pluck lily!

15. Dakshan's Sacrifice!

The fire, the Sun, the Moon, the god of death, Ravana and Andakan, the red-eyed Hari, Ayan and Indhran also, then the Good Dakshan of old and Echchan too, all lost their honour. Let us sing the glory of His wrath and pluck the lily!

16. Let us sing His wounds!

He is the rider on the mighty warring bull and He is the warring Lion of Shivapuram. In grace, He ate sweet cakes in earthly Madurai. The Pandyan King by means of whipping with a rod made Him to serve him. Let us sing the song of how He got the wound and pluck the lily!

17. He entered my frame!

The Gods of Heaven, the demons and even the ancient Vishnu and Brahman did not know the way to worship His sacred, golden Feet. But He is the One and He entered my frame and made me His own too. Let us sing His countless jewels of snake and pluck the lily!

18. I yearn for His anklet-Feet!

I am His slave and while I am seized with an endless longing to hear the sound of the mighty anklets of His glorious, sacred Feet and rejoice, He, the Lord of Perunthurai, dances in the Car-filled streets. So, let us sing of His great rapture and pluck the lily!

19. He became a baby too!

He is that Lord of Perunthurai who killed an elephant and wore its skin as His garment. He is the one who took the form of a mad. He became an infant too on earth. He is the Bounteous Lord of Uttharakosamangai. He is the Primal source of the ones who have been liberated. We sing of how He entered our hearts and let us pluck the lily!

20. He made me to serve Him!

He mounted a Horse with an easy and refined motion and entered Madurai city. He is the Lord of Perunthurai with a lustrous and divine Form. He came as a King and commanded us to do odd jobs for Him, and blessed us. Let us sing and praise His jewelled flower-feet and pluck the lily!

14. Thiruwunthiyar
(Victory over Spiritual Wisdom or Athma Gnanam)

PLAY OF WUNTHI!

1. The forts were burnt!

A great uproar and disturbance prevailed then, when the bow was bent, ready for war. The triple Forts were shattered to pieces and they were all burnt together immediately.

2. Even One Arrow was too many!

We did not catch sight of two arrows in Ekambam's own hands. A single arrow to destroy three cities, but even this One arrow was too many!

3. The axle broke!

The Car was brought and when He stamped His Foot to get into it, the axle broke. Sing and fly Wunthi! the three forts were gone!

4. He saved the Triod!

Who could aim His arrow to Him and save the three

who deserved life—fly Wunthi! Sing and fly Wunthi, the spouse of the tender breasted Dame, Umadevi.

5. The rout of devas!

The sacrifice was upset when charged. The Gods fled the place. Sing and fly Wunthi to the Lord who is Rudhra—Fly Wunthi!

6. Mal (Vishnu) was saved!

Sing and fly Wunthi for sacred Mal who ate offerings did not die that day but He lived. He is the father of the four-faced One, Brahman. Sing and fly Wunthi!

7. Fire-God lost His hands!

The dreadful God of Fire gathered it to swallow it up. But His hands were cut off. And the rites were all spoiled. Sing and fly Wunthi!

8. Ignore Dakshan!

Parvathi was then attacked by Dakshan with enmity. My dear, why should He be seen? Fly Wunthi! Fly Wunthi for that spouse of the Fair breast maid!

9. Indhra became a Kuyil!

Purandharan assumed the form of a beautiful kuyil and perched himself upon a tree. Sing and fly Wunthi!

10. Vyathiram lost his head!

Vyathiramar, in order to snap off births which chase, performed sacrifice which was full of spite and so lost his head, sing and fly Wunthi!

11. Placed a goat's head!

A goat's head was placed in place of Dakshan's head. Sing of this and fly Wunthi; stand with heaving breasts and fly Wunthi!

12. Began lost his eyes!

Began when he went to eat, ran to hide himself, but his eyes were plucked off! Fly Wunthi! to wipe off all our births too.

13. Saraswathi's loss!

Nagamagal's nose and Brahman's head were both nipped off. The Moon's own face too was crushed. Fly Wunthi that our ancient deeds might die!

14. Brahman's way of escape!

When the Chief of the sacrifice died, one of the four Vedas also sought to escape. Fly Wunthi! within the sacrifice of Indhra.

15. The Sun's loss of teeth!

The rows of teeth of Sun's red mouth were hit and broken to pieces. Sing and fly Wunthi! for the sacrifice too broke up.

16. Dakshan's loss of head!

On the day of the sacrifice, Dakshan lost his head although all his children stood round him and the sacrifice also collapsed. Sing and fly Wunthi!

17. His gift of Milk-Sea to the Babe!

He gave that Baby a Sea of Milk that day, He is the One

with beautiful braid locks, and is the Father of Kurman Himself. Fly Wunthi!

18. Brahman's loss of head!

A head of the four-faced One (Brahman) who sits on
Good lotus was then quickly nipped off by His sharp nail.
Fly Wunthi!

19. Ravana's loss!

Ravana stopped His car and tried to raise the Mount
Kailash. But all his ten heads and twenty hands too were
crushed. Sing and fly Wunthi!

20. The sages' flight in Ether!

Shiva safeguards the sky, for fear the plaidless sages lose
their way when in flight in the Ether. He even safeguards
beyond that too. Sing and fly Wunthi!

15. Thirutthonokkam (Purification of the Universe)

PLAY OF SHOULDER PEEP!

1. I am disillusioned!

I thought that this was the water of the flower tank. I was deluded then, for without knowledge, I sought to draw water from that mirage. Oh! You, who prefers dance in the Court of Bright Thillai, You, removed such illusions. I try to reach Your Red Feet, Thonokkam!

2. Let us sing the glory of Thillai's Lord!

He has made us His for fear that we should sink down in endless births and deaths. Hari, the calf thrower of the fruit and Brahman too do not know Him at the sacred court of Thillai with endless fame. Maids with clustering locks praise His goodness and we play Thonokkam!

3. Saint Kannappar's glory!

That loving woodman of thrilling frame with sandal feet, carried water in his mouth and offered flesh in worship. The mode of prayer shone like pure worship sanctioned by the scriptures and so he stands revealing greatness and was well blessed by God. Let us sing and play Thonokkam!

4. His grace is the talk of the town!

In order to thrill and melt my stony heart, He entered my soul with love like One who stood with mercy. It is the talk of the town that He placed me here on the righteous path to which all the world is witness too. Sing of this and let us play Thonokkam!

5. His eight-fold body!

He stood in all the eight-fold forms as earth, fire, water and wind, as the great Ether, Moon and the Sun and sense-owned souls. He is the only one who stands revealed as the seven-fold world, and as the ten directions. Singing all this we play Thonokkam!

6. With Shiva in heart our acts are divine!

There are many faiths with false meaning like Buddhism. Each one stands bewildered and confused in his own creed itself. He made the soul itself Shiva and so all its acts are now divine. With the mercy of that Father, let us play Thonokkam!

7. Chandeswara's Supreme Act!

Chandeswara, young guiltless bachelor, made offerings to Lord Shiva, He cut off both legs of a Brahmin who was his father because he destroyed the offerings which he had made to Shiva. Through Shiva, Esan's grace, this sin became a virtue which was praised by the Gods.

8. We have lost sense and honours!

Oh! Good maids, since we are lost in thought of the anklet Feet of Tennan, which are praised by heaven, we have lost all sense of pride and forgot reasoning too. If we could but have the grace of the rapture dancer we too could dance in rapture thus. Let us play Thonokkam!

9. Devas galore!

Since the time when those three demons who had escaped the fire and stood as guards at the gates of our own three-eyed Father, countless number of Indhras and Brahmans and Vishnus in plenty have perished on Earth. We play Thonokkam!

10. Mal's sacrifice and reward!

Vishnu had taken a thousand lotus flowers to worship Him. But, when he found that he was one short of thousand, he plucked out his own eye and then offered it to the rare, red feet of Haran. Sankaran, Our Lord, blessed Vishnu with a Disc (Sudharsana Disc). Singing this, we play Thonokkam!

11. Punishment of rebel devas!

Kaman lost his body, Kalan lost his life and the burning Sun too lost his teeth. The maiden tongue lost Her (Saraswathi) nose and Brahman lost one of His four heads. The fire lost His hand, the Moon, its crescent and Dakshan and Echchan their heads. They got His grace, we play Thonokkam!

12. The flame at Arunachalam!

Due to their mighty ignorance, both Brahman and Hari, each asserted that He was the Supreme. And Haran, in order to crush their soaring pride, stood there at Arunachalam as the transcendent flame, Measureless and Supreme. Singing this we play Thonokkam!

13. I was ploughing the arid field!

I, the poorest slave, have been born for a very long time, watering the wild and barren lands without worshipping Him who is the Lord of Lords. He is the First of all sages and He is the deathless Gem. He came and uprooted my birth. Singing this we play Thonokkam!

14. I am blest with release!

He is the Inner light, the worthiest One who cannot be described in words. When He entered my soul, I crossed the shoreless Sea of mighty lust. And the five vulture-senses which are not fed, flew in utter fear without a support. We sing of this and we play Thonokkam!

16. Thirupponoosal
(The Sacred Golden Swing)

1. His rare grace!

Let us all climb with joy upon the beautiful plank of gold, which has precious coral for its legs and strings of corals for its cord. In His kindness, He bestowed His fresh flower-feet, which Narayanan does not know, upon my dog-like self, so that I refuge, He is the rare nectar of Uttharakosamangai. Oh! You quarrelling maids, with dart-like eyes, let us sing His gracious Feet and move the golden swing!

2. He tastes delicious!

He has triple glittering eyes. The deathless Gods who live in heaven have themselves not caught sight of His flower-like Feet at all. He dwells like honey within my flesh and He tastes deliciously sweet. He melts me, for within me, He surges like Ambrosia's distilled essence. He is the King of Uttharakosamangai, Idaimaruthur is His Shrine. Oh! You, maids as beautiful as pea-hens and Your walk as graceful as swan, sing and move the golden swing!

3. His preference for me!

He has neither an end nor beginning. He, the Lord Shiva, in grace gave His sacred ashes to me alone, even while groups of mighty saints in hundreds and the heavenly ones in crores were standing near. He is the Supreme Gem who stands while I enjoy in His mighty flood of mercy. Let us, Oh! You, maids of golden-jewelled breasts, sing of the Gem-set, bright-domed mansions of Uttharakosamangai, and move the golden swing!

4. He lives in His serf's heart!

The poison-throated one is the master of the heavenly ones. Along with the maid of sweet words, He reached the cloud-spread mansions of Gems of Uttharakosamangai. He entered the hearts of His servants and He dwells there, welling up like nectar and shows them mercy. He has cut the chains of births and deaths. Let us sing of His pure, good praise. Oh! You, maids adorned with white bangles, sing and move the golden swing!

5. He is unknowable!

The twins did not know if He is male, or neuter or female. He ate the poison as His food, so that the hordes of gods might live and thrive without alarms, and He made them His in His own grace. He is the dancer of Uttharakosamangai, who is crowned with the crescent moon. Let us all sing of His excellences and let us worship Him. You, maids of breasts adorned with gold, sing and move the golden swing!

6. He fondled dog-like me!

He shares His form with His spouse. That King of Uttharakosamangai wears golden-dusted flowers on His braid. Even in the midst of His band of saints, He fondled dog-like me and enslaved me. He cuts away my births and He makes me shine without the ills of my old births! You, maids of breasts adorned with flowers, let us sing with melting love of His pair of dangling, bright earrings, and move the golden swing!

7. He cuts off the bonds!

That mighty one of the four Vedas shone brightly and stayed in Uttharakosamangai which is too precious for thought. He snaps away the bonds of sin of those who often sing His praise and bow in worship. We sing the charms of my own father and Lord. Just as the pretty pea-hens dance on the swans, You, the maids with gold-like breasts, climb on to the planks and move the golden swing!

8. He rode a horse and graced us!

He descended from the heights of the grand mountain and consumed the love of enough men on this earth. Rising from the depths of the Seas, He filled the world and rode a horse and made us all His own. It is so hard for Mal to reach where He dwells in sacred Uttharakosamangai where all virtues shine. Let us sing His fame in full-mouthed strain with joy and melting hearts and move the golden swing!

9. He made us His serfs!

In quite a lustrous, peerless form, He came in grace to dwell in sacred Uttharakosamangai which is surrounded by coco-palm groves. He snapped away my births and made all men like me His slaves. His braid is fragrant with the cassia flowers. With His partner-maid, He received all our homage. Let us sing His worth, You, Maids of heaving jewelled breasts, and move the golden swing!

17. Annaippatthu (The Ten Verses of the Motherhood)

1. The Lord of Lords!

His word is the Veda; His ashes are white and His form is rosy. Oh Mother! Nada is His drum; she says, the Lord whose drum is the Nada is the Lord of Brahman, the four-faced One and Vishnu!

2. Dweller of the soul!

His eyes are painted black. He is a Sea of mercy. Oh! Mother, He dwells and melts in souls. He dwells in souls and melts and gives rapturous tears which are endless in their eyes.

3. The Eternal Groom!

He is the Eternal bridegroom. He is of perfect beauty. Oh! Mother, she says, He dwells in Hearts. He who dwells in hearts is Tenna, the Rapturous one and the Father of Perunthurai.

4. He unsatiated sight!

Oh Mother, she says, His form is so wondrous and He adorns Himself with a snake as jewel, skin as His garment and He smears Himself with ashes. The more and more I see His wondrous Form, the more my heart withers away. Why is it, Oh Mother? she says.

5. The giver and the controller!

His arms are long, His braids are closely knit, Oh! Mother, she says, He belongs to goodly Pandiland. That Lord of goodly Pandiland subdues the wandering mind and He shows His love. Oh Mother! she says.

6. The unseen one!

He is of the glorious Uttharakosamangai which is hard to think of. Oh Mother, she says, He dwells within my heart. Oh! Mother, she says, it is wonder that He dwells within my heart, where both Brahman and Vishnu cannot see!

7. The prayerful one!

His master is white and the skull in His hand is white. He wears a cloak which is prayer. Oh Mother! she says, that the One who wears a prayer-cloak mounts a speedy horse and He takes my heart captive.

8. The Lord of music!

He wears the Aruhu tali and sandalpaste, He makes us His own slaves, Oh Mother, she says, it is wondrous that the palms of that Adigal who made us all His slaves, contain a pair of tinkling symbols.

9. My heart melts!

Umadevi's partner who has taken the form and disguised Himself as an ascetic comes begging here, Oh Mother! why is it my heart withers away the moment He, who comes begging, goes away from me.

10. He gives frenzy!

His crown is adorned with Cassia flowers, with the moon, with vilva leaves and phrenzy. Oh Mother! Why is it that the phrenzy flowers that He wears on His crown cause a great frenzy in me today.

18. Kuyilppatthu (The Ten Verses of the Kuyil)

1. Shiva's Crown and the Feet!

Listen You, Oh! Kuyil, of pleasing voice: Far beyond the seven deep worlds dwell the Truthful twin Feet of our Lord. It is beyond all speech to speak of His bright Gem-set crown. He has no origin, quality or end. Call Him to come!

2. His grace to Mandodhari!

All the beautiful seven-fold worlds highly praise Him. Every form is His form. The Lord of Perunthurai bestowed His mighty gracious bliss upon Mandodhari of southern Lanka which is surrounded by Sea. Oh Kuyil! With Your blessed voice, call that King of South Pandi!

3. His capital shrine!

Oh! Kuyil, Your colour is sky blue. The Lord resides with His tender Dame, Umadevi within the shrine of Utthara-kosamangai town which shines with great beauty of gem-set of high mansions and which is rich in fine virtues, to cause the world to shine. Call Him to come!

4. He prefers the earth and men!

Oh Tiny Kuyil! in ripened juicy fruit groves hear this: The Lord of plenty scorning heaven entered the earth and made Men His own. He scorned the body and entered my heart and there he dwells as mystical knowledge in me. He is the bridegroom of the maid whose eyes do scorn the fawn. Call Him to come to us!

5. He is unknown to the three!

Oh lovely Kuyil! of Joy! He came down to earth from heaven just like the Sun of radiant rays and killed the desires of His saints. The triple gods—the first, the middle and the end do not know the great red feet of that grand warrior. Call Him to come here!

6. He rides a horse!

Oh Kuyil, that twitters on the boughs, I will give you joy. He is the Rapture from where all ambrosia springs, the loving One who rules the seven worlds. He is that God from heaven and is that rider who comes upon a horse and that is bright with tints of gold and gems. Call Him to come here!

7. He is all the three Tamil kings!

Oh Kuyil! I will pet you, I will also be your helpful mate. His purest form eclipses gold and He shines in beauteous glory. He is the King and bounteous Lord of Perunthurai who rode a horse. He is all the three Tamil Kings such as Pandi, Chera, Chozha and Buyangan. Call Him to come here!

8. He is Light unknown to the two!

Oh Tender Kuyil! You come and listen here. While Vishnu and Brahman, the four-faced one searched and stooped and stood in thought that true one, the rider on the prancing steed and of flowing braid, shot forth as a bright flame, split up and transcended the heavens as radiant light. Call Him to come here!

9. His lotus red form!

Oh You, Kuyil of bright, black colour who lives in fragrant groves, listen! His form is novel and shines like a glorious, red lotus. He showed His Feet on earth and cut off my bonds and made me His. He is that rare nectar who has a form of beautiful God. Call Him to come here!

10. He claimed me as His own!

Oh Kuyil! who chirps in the gardens filled with plenty of boughs and flowers, hear this! He came here as a sage and showed His Rosy Red Feet. He pointed to me and said that I was His kinsman and He made me His own in His own kindness. He has a sacred form like a red flame and is the Lord of Gods. Call Him to come here!

19. Thirutthasangam (The Sacred Ten Insignia)

1. His name!

Oh! Tender, fair and rare parrot! Will You now pronounce with distinctness the glorious, sacred names of our own Lord of Perunthurai as the Lord of Arur and as the red-hued Lord? Brahman and Vishnu themselves pronounce Him as their Lord and the King of Gods.

2. His Kingdom!

Oh! Parrot of green emerald! Your words are sweet and flawless. You must speak of the land of the King of the seven-fold world and ours. You must know for certain that Pandiland is the kingdom of the One who takes in love and bestows endless release on His saints.

3. His Capital City!

Oh! Parrot of the flowery, fragrant groves, tell us which is the town wherein Shiva who is the partner of Umadevi and ruler of all of us dwells. His town is Uttharakosamangai which saints celebrate much and which is considered by them as Shivapuram on earth.

4. His River!

Oh! Blessed bird, one so fine, with green wings and red mouth, name the river of Shiva of Perunthurai within our hearts. Oh! maid, look! the rapture which descends to clean the dirt of the mighty souls is only the river of our own Lord Shiva.

5. His Mountain!

Oh! You, parrot with purple-red mouth, we pray you, tell us the Mountain of the beautiful one of deathless Perunthurai. Look! His mountain is the one that spreads its light and drives the mental darkness away and grants in kindness the salvation of bliss.

6. His Courser!

Oh! my parrot, come here and speak. Do not search for your cage. You must tell us now on what the famous, peer-less one rides. While the heavenly maids of honey-like hearts sing His glorious praise, He with rapture rides upon the heavenly Ether which is His steed.

7. His offensive weapon!

Oh! parrot, your words are as sweet as honey in the combs that hang up upon the boughs. Tell us what weapon the pure King of Perunthurai wields to conquer foes. In His hand, He wields the Trishul which pierces through the three "dirts" and melts the purest hearts of those who seek refuge in Him.

8. His drum!

Oh! parrot of sweet milk-like words tells us what is that drum that roars loud within the presence of the King of Perunthurai. His drum is the mighty Nada which roars with infinite bliss and which frightens and drives away the foes of births.

9. His favourite garlands!

Oh! parrot of the choicest words, tell us that true garlands, He, of Perunthurai and Lord of saints of love, wears. The master who is guarding a dog-like me against the evil deeds, delights Himself in wearing the good Tali-Arughu garlands.

10. His Banner!

Oh! parrot of the green groves, mention the beautiful flag that shines in wondrous honour of the King of Perunthurai surrounded by sweet water. His spotless banner of the bull shines high above and flutters in great terror within the hearts of the enemies.

20. Thiruppalliezhuchi (The Song of Rousing from the Sacred Couch)

1. He is the source of life!

Oh! Being, I praise You. You are the source of all my life. It has now dawned. Through the lustre that is shed by Your beautiful smile, from Your bright face, that blooms for us in love. We worship Your twin flower-feet, decking them with clustering wreaths of flowers. Oh Lord Shiva! You dwell in the sacred Perunthurai which is surrounded with cooling paddy fields wherein the lotus flowers bloom. You have a lengthy, bull-banner and offer You myself too. Our Lord! rise up from Your couch and grant us Your grace.

2. He is the mount of rapture!

Arunan, that is the Sun, has reached the East and so the darkness has fled and gone. Like the rising Sun of mercy, Your flower-like face while rising, Your beautiful eyes when they open resemble the fragrant flowers when they blossom and shine. Just like the pair of eyes of men, swarms of bees in different rows come and hum. Lord Shiva! You dwell in Perunthurai. You are the Sea of waves, rise up from Your couch and grant us joy.

3. He is affable to us!

The beautiful Kuyils have chirped their notes and the cocks too have already crowed. The different birds have also sung aloud and the conches too are blown. The light of the stars has gone away and now the rising Sun has emerged. Oh! God be pleased with us. Lord Shiva who dwells in sacred Perunthurai, You are too difficult for all to know. But You are friendly to us. Our Lord! rise up from Your couch and grant us Your love.

4. His diverse devotees!

Those players who play on sweet-tuned lutes and lyres stand there. Those who chant the Rigveda and sing the psalms stand here. Those with close-knit flower wreaths in their palms stand there. Those who worship and those who weep and those who faint stand here. Those whose palms are clasped above their heads, adoring You, stand there. Lord Shiva You dwell in the sacred Perunthurai, make me Yours and show me Your sweetest grace. Oh! Our Lord, awake, rise up from Your couch and grant us Your mercy.

5. We do not know those who have seen Him!

The poets performing dances have sung in pleasing tunes that You dwell in every element and that You have neither exit or advent. Except for this only, we have not seen, or known or heard at all of those who have seen You. You are the King of the sacred Perunthurai of cooling paddy fields, You are rare and uncommon for us even to think of You. You manifest Yourself before our eyes and kill our woes and in grace, You make us Yours. Our Lord! awake and rise up from Your couch and grant us Your bliss.

6. Men worship Him with maid-like attitude!

Your saints who are free from distractions live in peace and so they know Your self. There are men who are rid of their bonds and those like them also come as human beings and as the maids with painted eyes to worship You. You are the spouse of the divine Umadevi, Lord Shiva who dwells in the sacred Perunthurai surrounded with cooling paddy fields, where purple lotus flowers bloom, cut away this birth and make me Yours in loving kindness. Our Lord awake and rise up from Your couch and grant us Your kindness.

7. Though rare for gods He is affable to us!

The gods themselves do not know that He is that taste of fruits, that He is the nectar, that He is friendly and that He is too difficult to know. But, You came in grace and made us Yours, so that makes us to say that Yours is the sacred form, and that You are the one that is One. You reside at Uttharakosamangai encircled with honied groves. You, the King of sacred Perunthurai, tell us of serving You and we will all obey. Our Lord! wake up and rise up from Your couch and grant us Your peace.

8. He visits His humble serfs' abodes!

You are the ancient First, You are the middle and You are the end of all and everything ends in You. When the three Gods themselves do not know You, who else could know You? You are the Lord who in grace paid Your visit to all the ancient huts of all Your slaves, along with Umadevi of soft fingers. You revealed Your sacred form which resembles red fire. You revealed also Your dwelling place which is sacred Perunthurai. You showed Your sage-form too and made me Your own. Oh You, rare nectar, rise up from Your couch and grant us Your goodness.

9. He caused His saints to live on earth!

You are the Supreme Being whom the Gods themselves in heaven cannot even approach. But You have made Your own slaves who have served You, come to this world and live in bliss. You belong to the rich and sacred Perunthurai, You are delighted honey that lives within our eyes who are Your lineal slaves. You are ambrosia that springs out from the Sea. You are like sugarcane who lives within the thoughts of saints who love You. You are the soul of all the worlds. Our Lord! rise up from Your couch and grant us Your self.

10. Even Mal and Ayan seek this Earth due to Him!

The sacred Brahman and Vishnu the One who reclines on flower realize that their days are wasted for they have not gone to the earth to be born on it, which Shiva uses to save the souls of all. Every God in heaven longs for life upon this earth. Oh! My Lord who dwells in the sacred Perunthurai, You have made us all serve You as Your own saints. Oh You, rare Ambrosia, rise up from Your couch and grant us Your blessings.

21. Kovil Mootha-thiruppathigham (The Ancient Temple-Hymn)

1. Place me amidst Your saints!

Your mistress dwells in Your own company and You dwell in the company of Your mistress. If both of You together dwell in me, then I, Your servant, should forever dwell in the company of Your loving saints. Oh! Primal Lord of Endlessness, do stand before me and bestow Your grace so that my wish might be fulfilled.

2. Tarry a while and take me!

In the past, You stood before me and made me Your own. Though I too continued in Your service, I was left behind. My Lord! You pleased us with Your dance in the Golden court of Thillai. If You do not wait for me a little while and if You do not stand by me and do not ask me to come, will not the saints who do not know me, ask You, who I am?

3. I will appeal to the world!

You are pleased with the service of those who love You.

You, the perfect source in the golden court, gave life and grace to those who offered sacrifices and sought Your way. So, if I of hard, unmelting heart should plead my cause before the world, won't they say that it is not just, I shall die if You refuse to show Your grace.

4. Make me not despair!

You are the perfect source. You are the ancient source of the five senses, the three gods and of myself too. You are the source who makes all Your ancient saints to meet in heaven. Oh King of the golden court, what else I do except to wonder and weep in despair, if You would not in grace pity me at all.

5. You are the Ghee in curd to me!

Like the patient heron watching and waiting its prey, I waned by day and by night with the load of worries and looked up for Your grace crying and calling You, Nectar and dancing King of the golden court. If You showed Yourself only to the liberated saints of bliss, and if You were silent to me, like ghee in curd, won't men revile at You?

6. They scorn me!

Some people swear at me and call me names. While all the rest of them speak of me scornfully as Your servant, Oh! Bright One, I stand and yearn for Your Good grace alone. Hence, Oh! Father and Esa of the golden court, in pity grant that I worship Your audience hall filled with Your lovers.

7. Shepherdless cow!.

When in distress, I stood and cried and said that the dancer at the golden court will pity us, then You came and made me Yours and taught me rare truths. Shall I be a shepherdless cow, still. You are our life. So in Your kindness, call me to reach the place wherein Your chosen saints and You dwell and sport in mirth.

8. I pine in anguish!

If You deny Your grace, to me, then who is here to tell me not to fear. You are gold to use, the dancer in the court of the gold. You cared for me and entered me and made me Your own. Parting from You, I now pine in anguish! Won't everyone laugh if You call me but do not show me Your band of kind saints and make me one in their company.

9. Your saints enjoy!

Your gracious band of saints are filled with joy and so laugh. Their delight is as if they have tasted honey. They mingle in groups themselves and explain Your own sacred scriptures. They listen to Your sacred texts and praise You highly. They in groups repeatedly pronounce Your Holy name and call on You as the dancing King of the golden court. Oh Nambi, shall I, a dog-like, an evil one before them. Hence, grant me Your mighty grace.

10. I rave Your name!

I thought that You won't fail to bestow Your grace upon me and so I raved about wildly calling Your name, with tears brimming my eyes and with a faltering tongue, bowing and pensive, praising You and with a melting heart, I often thought of You. My Lord, pity me and bless my withering soul adorning Your court of Gold.

22. Kovil Thiruppathigham (The Sacred Temple-Lyric)

1. Disclose Your true-self!

You blocked the channels of the five treacherous senses which perversely hallucinated me. You are the fountain of ambrosia within my heart and You rose as the Supreme Light. Oh! distilled honey and Shiva of sacred Perunthurai, come and grace, show Your truest self. You are the mighty bliss that knows no end and that transcends all dwelling places. You are my love personified!

2. I have nothing to give in return!

You granted me sweet bliss even beyond my worth who is Your slave so that my soul and body mellowed and melted with great blissful rapture. I have nothing with me to give You in return for this. You are the Ever free who spreads as all things. You are before, behind and the endless source of all things. You, of South Perunthurai, my Lord Shiva, are the King of glorious Shivapuram too.

3. Make me describe Your self!

You are the King and the master to me who is the slave of Your servants and saints. You entered and lived in me, softening and melting my whole soul and every pore of my body. You are the light of truth dispelling all darkness of life. Oh Shiva! You dwell in sacred Perunthurai. You stand forth as knowledge of spiritual mysteries which is beyond all words and thoughts. You can be known only by this spiritual knowledge. So, teach me this knowledge to describe You.

4. I have no more to worry!

The sages well-versed in sacred knowledge, the heavenly ones and all the rest cannot in any way understand You, the rare being. You are the peerless one and the soul of all souls. You are our own Balm which cures me of my birth-disease. You are the subtle, spotless ether shining in the middle of the dense darkness. Oh Shiva, who dwells in sacred Perunthurai, You are the bliss who is devoid of all qualities. Henceforth, I have nothing to grieve for here, since I have well reached You.

5. I have no more to beg to You!

You are the fulness of Unlimited powers which cannot decrease. You are the sweet ambrosia without flaws. You are a mount of endless flame which is luxuriant. You are the Vedas themselves and also the essence of the Vedas too. Oh! Shiva, who dwells in sacred Perunthurai! Oh King, You came and lived in my heart, and flowed within my soul like a bound burst stream. What more shall I beg of You in future!

6. I satiated my eyes with Your vision today!

While I beg and pray and melt in heart, You emerge slowly within my soul as the splendorous light. Oh Shiva! who dwells in sacred Perunthurai! Your own lotus Feet red of colour, shine upon the crowns of gods. You are the limitless ether, water, fire, wind and earth and yet, You are not all these. You are the Form that is concealed in all of them. I rejoice because today I have seen and fixed my eyes on You.

7. None can know You!

You gave me grace today and so dispelled my darkness. Like the rising Sun, You dwell in my soul, with ceaseless thought, I thought about Your true nature. They approach nearer and nearer and wearing off atom by atom, become one with You, nothing else subsists except You. Oh Siva, who dwells in sacred Perunthurai shrine, You are none of these at all and nothing subsists without You. Who is there, who can know You all?

8. Who are my kinsmen?

You are that expanse of light that stems up and spreads as the earth and heaven and all the rest of things. You are the pure One too hard for thought, for You are the fire in water too. Oh! You are that sweet honey which springs within the hearts of those who are filled with Your own flood of grace. Oh Shiva! who dwells in sacred Perunthurai say who are all my kinsmen here and who are my aliens? You are the Jyothi which gives me great ecstasy.

9. Sacred mount of grace!

You are the formless one, You are the form of that resplendent light which was seen. You are the first, the middle and the last who is so hard to describe or paint with mere words alone. You are the Sea of mighty bliss which can wash away my earthly bonds. You are the sacred mount of grace and goodness without evil. Having come and blessed me with Your pair of Feet, how can You in fairness leave me? Speak with grace, Oh Lord Shiva! who dwells in sacred Perunthurai!

10. I have nothing to give in return for Your bliss!

What You have given to me is Your goodself, what You have got is my self. Oh Sankara! do speak and say, who is cleverer of the two, I have well gained from You the rapture-bliss that knows no end. Is there even a single thing that You have got from me? Our Lord, You have converted my heart as Your holy shrine, Oh Father and Esa! You have made my body Your dwelling place. Oh Shiva! who dwells in the sacred Perunthurai, I have nothing to give to You in return for all these You have given to me.

23. Chethilappatthu (The Decade of Despondency)

1. I know now what to do!

Your fresh and flower-like Feet entered my soul which is full of lies and caused my heart to melt and swell with nectar that is sweet. Though I have now parted from them, my deceitful self is not yet dead and even I in my wakefulness have not lost the goal of my own soul. Oh! Teacher and the King, You are the mighty Sea of grace, the father whom both Brahman and Vishnu could not catch sight of at all. Oh Lord Shiva! who dwells in the sacred Perunthurai, You are the God of red form, I do not know how, and what is to be done now.

2. Still I wander here!

The gods and all the rest, with the growth of anthills and trees upon their bodies and with water and air for their food, became reduced to bones, but could not perceive Your flower-like Feet. Oh King! You captured me by dropping a single word alone in me. But yet, I do not tremble, not does my heart melt. Oh! Shiva, who dwells in the sacred Perunthurai, I feel no love for You at all. I still roam and wander and have not yet destroyed this loveless body of mine.

3. I was drunk with Your grace!

You considered even my base self worthy and so bestowed Your grace on me. And I being thus blessed became quite exultant and walked the earth head-over-heels. You, rider on bull, Sankara! are the basis of the countless heavenly ones. You, Eternal One, You ate the poison from the Sea of waves. You are the bowman who destroyed the forts of Your enemies. Oh! Shiva, who dwells in the sacred Perunthurai, I pray that my deceitfulness be dead and gone.

4. Why did You thrall me!

Why did you make my self Your own, while Brahman and Vishnu, Your devotees who perform rare penances with love and such harsh rigours, while those whose hearts dissolving, melt like wax on fire, and those with bony-bodies all think of You alone and stand and wait for You. But my mind is like the hard knur of the knotty parai tree, my eyes dry like wood and my ears harder than steel. Oh Shiva, who dwells in the sacred Perunthurai, You are the King of South Perunthurai and of Shivaloka.

5. Rid me of this illusionary frame!

I kept myself away from gods who drag fateward and cried aloud in love to You as father, and now I follow Your own gractious ways. You are the Rarest Being whom the gods of earth too cannot reach. Oh King! please grant me Your grace of not parting You at all and show me Your jewelled Feet. Show me Your own grace and command me to be rid of all illusions about this perishable body. Oh Shiva, who dwells in the sacred Perunthurai, You are the Supreme God of gods and are above the pettiest of the gods.

6. I cannot endure my separation from You!

I have neither cut and split my body into bits nor have I plunged myself within the fire for not having known the ways of Your grace. I cannot bear life in this body which is perishable, nor have I any other place of refuge to go to. My Lord of warring bull, I always keep on praising You. Being separated and living far from You, I have not yet sought death. What shall I do? Oh Lord Shiva! who dwells in the sacred Perunthurai, surrounded with paddy-fields wherein the water stands embanked. In loving grace, command me to do such and such a thing.

7. Show Your Supreme Way!

Oh! Heavenly Lord, You are full of sportful guiles, for You, my blue-throated nectar that ate the poison from the billowed Sea. Neither would my dog-like self ever think of You in love nor would my friend-like self ever sing and pray 'Namashivaya', and bow before Your Feet. Yet show me Your supreme way, Oh Pingnakan! Upon whose braid rests the crescent moon. If I raved like a stranger, would it ever become You, Oh! Shiva, who dwells in the sacred Perunthurai.

8. Does my grief please You?

While Ayan who sits on flower and Vishnu who sleeps on the Sea of dashing waves, and while Purandharan and all the rest of the gods themselves wait, You purge and clean me of my sins and show me Your bejewelled Feet. My balm, when I despaired much and knew not what was to be done, You asked me to hold fast to the goal and placed me within the midst of Your saints. Does it please Yourself that I, Your slave, should grieve with pain? Oh Lord Shiva! You dwell in the sacred Perunthurai which is encircled with paddy-fields full of cool water.

9. Bid me reach Your Feet!

The mortals, Indhra, the four-faced Brahman and the heavenly ones all stood in despair, when You loved me and made me Your own. Your flower-feet took away the life from the God of death. You owned the Ganges and held fire in your palms. Order me too with eyes like wood to reach You and then catch sight of Your own flower feet for which Vishnu waits and raves to see. Oh Shiva! You dwell in the sacred Perunthurai surrounded with paddy-fields which are so full of fishes and flowers.

10. I was bewildered!

You came with great tenderness and in Your kindness asked me to come to You and drove away my fears. Yet I did not melt by plunging, or gathering and drinking from Your great, gracious Sea. Oh Shiva! who dwells in sacred Perunthurai, neither the one who handles the conch nor the God on flower knows You. I lost my joys and now stand bewildered solely by my griefs alone. Oh Great Ocean! You whose partner is the daughter of the mountain, You dwell on the mighty Mount of Kailash.

24. Adaikkalppatthu
(The Ten Verses of Refuge)

1. My only refuge!

The saints whose mellowed hearts are mellowed, reached and lived at Your red Feet which are like the clustering lotus-like flowers, are gone with You, while I, the sinful one, live in this mean body full of worms as an ill-taught slave of foul mind and faulty wisdom; and You alone are my master and refuge.

2. Your mighty greatness!

I always perform disgustful deeds, and through Your greatness, You forgive my meanness, You wear snakes and You subdue the rage of the turbulent Ganges on Your braid, By Your grace, You uproot my births, Oh My master, I, Your slave, seek refuge in You.

3. The rarest one!

Oh Mighty Lord! You uproot my births and give frenzied love. Oh! Clever Lord, You are the Lord who enters my heart, Both Vishnu and flower-god and the tall Brahman stood not knowing You, for You are the Lord who is indeed rare. You are my master, and I, Your slave, seek refuge in You.

4. You alone save!

Your own saints ascended up the Heavens with Your own Feet which they used as their raft, when they sank in floods from the clouds of griefs. I am also whirled within the Sea of troubles, dashed about by waves of women and bit by the sharks of lust, and I sink. Oh! My master, I, Your slave, seek a refuge in You.

5. The sole giver of grace!

I fell a prey to the wiles of maids with curly locks and thus forgot Your ways. Growing weak in body and mind, I still live in this dark body. Ah! You are the spouse of Her with eyes like startled fawn. Oh Lord of gods! I pray for grace. My master, I, Your slave, seek refuge in You.

6. You are my father!

I languish like the split up curd that bounds within the pot, when the maids with painted eyes like young mango churn with the rod. When and on what day shall I the sinful bow at Your Feet? My father, and master, I, Your slave, seek refuge in You who is like a Sea.

7. You pitied my faults!

I rolled in pain and was netted by the passions for the bright-eyed maids with thin waists. In Your kindness, You entered me, lest I should roll off. And tasting as sweet ambrosia, You distilled Yourself in my eyes. You, the fair-eyed Lord, pity my faults, for I, Your slave, seek refuge in You.

8. Command me to come to You!

My mind like a spindle within the warp hides and flies. So You, Oh spouse of the maid of eyes like young mango, will You call me unto Your Feet or drop me in hell. My Lord!

I die for I do not know Your purpose. I, Your slave, seek refuge in You.

9. Your feet are endless bliss!

The saints who did not part from You, came beneath Your gracious Feet and enjoyed the endless bliss. But I do not know how to worship You. In fact, I do not know You at all, as I have no wisdom with which I could know You too. My master, hence I seek refuge in You.

10. Your grace in honey-like water!

I gathered up the gracious ambrosia poured out by You with both my palms and quaffed it. Through fate, my sinful throat was choked. Give me as drink the limpid honey-like water and save me. Oh! My master, I grieve and I, Your slave, seek refuge in You.

25. Aasaippatthu
(The Ten Verses of Desire)

1. Please summon me!

Oh! Perfect Gem! You gave me as wealth Your red, jewelled Feet which the eagle-mannered one could not see, and made me Your own here. Won't You drive away my ignorance and call me to come to You. Oh! My father, Look, my soul yearns to gain Your grace from You.

2. I cannot brook life in frame!

I cannot endure to live within this queer body which has the skin as its coat, wherein muscles and bones have been concealed and which is stitched with milk-white nerves. Oh King! call me to come to You, You are my rare nectar which is beyond the reach of men of every land. Oh master, I yearned to see You. See Great Father!

3. Look at my face and bid me come!

Destroy this cottage, that is my body which is full of pus and dirt and filthy flies, and command me to come to You. Oh King and dancer! You are the Gem of a teacher who guards and makes me Your own. You are the God who is rare for the Gods themselves. Shiva call me to come to You

and look a while at my own face. See Great Father! I yearned
for this.

4. I suffer through this foul frame!

My body is a walking bone-built cell that is worthless
and that is stuffed with loathsome putrid pus. Hail to You,
my Lord! Looking at Your own light, I dissolve, soften and
melt and reach Your own sacred flower-feet. See Great Father! I yearned for this alone.

5. Tell me 'You are mercy'!

I lived like a ripe tamarind with my body who is Your
servant full of noisome flesh within and skin outside. You,
the ash-worn rider on the bull, are rare ambrosia which came
too easily and made me Yours. See Great Father, my soul
yearned to hear Your words saying that You are mercy itself
to me.

6. Take away this body given by You!

My dog-like self is very much tired. Henceforth, I cannot bear living here any more. Take back this birth given by
You of flower-red Feet which are unknown by the Gods. You
are my liberation. See master! and Great Father! I yearned for
a long time to see the lustrous rays and Your charming smile
on Your own countenance.

7. I'd chant Your thousand names!

You are the Supreme one whom earth and heaven adore
and worship, Supreme Light come. You come and make me
Yours and give me the eternal world. Great Father see, my
soul yearned to rave and roam about and chant out all Your
thousand names and worship You as my Lord and rare
Ambrosia.

8. I'd melt by crying Your name!

Behold Oh! King of Ayyaru and Great Father! my soul yearned to worship with my hands and embrace Your red jewelled Feet and then to place them both upon my head quite tirelessly and rave with my mouth as my Lord, our Lord! our own father and thus to melt like wax on fire.

9. I long for the sight of Your ancient saints!

Supreme God and father who is great and peerless one, see, that I, Your slave, yearned to cast away this painful body and be rid of its agonies. I longed, too, to enter the city of Shivapuram, to see Your splendorous, beautiful light and to feast my pair of eyes by seeing the band of Your own ancient saints.

10. Tell me not to fear!

I, a dog-like one, languish, for I am caught within the wrathful net of maids with fish-like, fire-like eyes. Oh! Light of Wisdom, I seek no help. You are the Spouse of the maid of fine and feather-like feet. Look, Oh great father, I yearned to hear speak with Your coral lips and tell me not to fear.

26. Athisayappatthu (The Ten Hymns of Wonder)

1. Oh, the Peerless One!

Oh! Supreme treasure and bright ruby, I have never before called You so or melted in heart, for I lay exhausted by my lust for the charms of maids with beautiful breasts. But never have I seen such wonder, the sacred feet of the father who has no comparison or equal. He has made me His and has placed me in the midst of His saints.

2. He has given me forgetfulness!

I neither think of all that is unjust and transient nor mingle with those who think of them. I sorrow, I whirl between the births and deaths. Have we seen such wonder that the Supreme Lord whose half is a maid and who lives as the first one eternally, has made me His and placed me in the midst of His saints.

3. He placed me among His saints!

My father of triple eyes, who is too hard for all to know but who is friendly to His saints, has placed the baby-moon upon His braid which is brighter than gold. We have never seen such wonder of His driving away my time-worn mighty sins and He, a God who like a mother placed me in the midst of His saints.

4. The worldlings call me mad!

Oh You! listen to this one reason why the worldlings call me mad. I did not know how to trust and tread the ways which lead to Your grace. I was ready to die and fall in hard hells, but You, my own Father, made me Your own and placed me in the midst of saints. Have we seen such a wonder!

5. I stand ruined!

I did not join Your saints in prayer nor worship You with varied flowers and I am now ruined, for I stood enslaved to the charms of maidens of fragrant locks. But have we seen such wonder of our Lord who dances with the fire and snake on His braid in nights and has made me His and placed me in the midst of His saints.

6. He came to me a sinner!

Due to my sins, I did not chant Your sacred name of five letters—NAMASHIVAYA, neither did I befriend those men of ancient wisdom nor lived a life of virtues. I was ready to be born on earth and die and become earth. Have we seen such wonder of my master who made me His and placed me in the midst of His saints.

7. The Unequalled One!

I considered this false cottage that is my body as real and permanent, which is full of holes, with a wall of flesh full of worms and dripping with pus. Since then, I was thrilled in a Sea of sorrow. But have we seen such wonder as that great master who is the perfect splendour of pearls, of gems, of corals and of diamonds, who made me His own and placed me in the midst of His saints.

8. He made me stainless!

He pushed me from His presence that day and dropped me in this body. But that bright splendour eyed me and instantly taught me subtle truths. He caught me with a yoke and lifted me and cut off my age-old sins and stains. He made me His own and placed me in the midst of His saints. Have we seen such wonder!

9. I find Him in me!

The truth that dwells within this body is the Supreme Being who is like the fragrance of the sweetest flower, a formless thing eluding grasp. Have we not seen such wonder of the father making me His own and placing me in the midst of His saints, for fear, I should follow the mad who do not see the truth, but enjoy worldly pleasures.

10. He showed me the truthful way!

I considered this body which is a tiny hut built of sin and raised in darkness as worthy. I rejoiced and rushed to fall in dark hells. But have you seen wonder of that Enlightening Red Fire which drove away my false ways and which graced me with that truthful way. It was that same red fire which at once powdered the three forts in an angry mood.

27. Punarchippatthu (The Ten Verses of Mystic Wedlock)

1. Mal and Brahman could not see Him!

When I, the least one, was pleased with a membership of the worthless gang, the Hill of lustrous gold, the unbored pearl and the Shrine of mercy made me His own servant. So, You are my rare nectar which Brahman and Vishnu were prevented from seeing, but which gave itself to me, Oh! When shall I thus be locked up with Him my perfect Gem in this mystical wedlock?

2. I would melt and worship Him!

Oh King! I, Your slave, cannot bear anymore. When I am not stuck up within the muddy slush of the five-fold senses found upon this earth, then I would think of You and pray You as Shiva and as my own Lord. I would also wail with a soft and melting heart, like the springs in the pure water sands. But when shall I be praying and thus be united with Him my perfect Gem in the mystic wedlock?

3. I would wail aloud and worship Him with flowers!

He is that lofty fire that shot up, which frightened the

tall Brahman and Vishnu. You are my rare nectar which made my loveless self Your slave. Before the good old saints, I would with a heart surging with love and by wailing loud to my heart's content strew sweet flowers and worship You. Oh! When shall I be locked up thus with Him my perfect gem in mystic wedlock?

4. He is all that is sweet!

You are Him, the mellowed Nelli fruit, whose name is mouthed and praised by lotus Brahman and Vishnu and all the rest. You are the light which is beyond the word and meaning. You are the sweet honey, the milk, the limitless nectar and its flower too. When shall I embrace You and thus be united with You my perfect Gem in mystic wedlock?

5. He made me His slave!

He is the great one with bright and gleaming feet and crown which both Brahman and Vishnu by digging down in the earth and soaring high up in the sky could not see. You claimed my service as Your servant and made the whole world know of it. You are full of love which made You call me to come to You. When shall I praise all that and thus be locked up with You, my perfect gem, in mystic wedlock?

6. I would worship Him with thrill and tears!

Though, He came before in this wide world and graced me with tenderness and with His own great rapture, I left Him for, I was much bewildered in this wide world. I want to speak of all this with joy and love, with tears streaming and with water surging in my body which gets thrilled. Oh! When shall I with deep devotion dwell with my perfect gem in mystic wedlock?

7. I would worship Him with closed palms and flowers!

He is the fire, the water, the wind and the earth, He is the Ether who is too hard for the thought of strangers, He is the unique one who is unequalled. Seeing Him with thrill and joy and then, roaring with my vibrant throat, shedding tears from my eyes and clasping both my palms when shall I deck Him with flowers and dwell in the mystic nuptial with the perfect Gem?

8. I would dance and stare at His Form!

To gaze at His true form which is sacred and which is like the red evening sky, I would be thrilled and thrilled with dissolved bones, melting heart, standing, sitting, falling, rising, laughing, weeping, worshipping, praising and dancing in all different ways. When shall I enter and stand and dwell with my perfect gem in mystic wedlock?

9. Day and night I will worship Him with flowers!

You are the father and the mother of the triple seven-fold worlds. You are the simpleton who made my own dog-like self Your slave. You are the rare Balm for all the ills of our births. You are the gem of the knowledge of spiritual mysteries, from where the divine honey drips always, praising You thus by day and by night, when shall I search You for, and reach Your own beautiful pair of flower-like feet. Oh! When shall I dwell in mystic wedlock with my perfect gem?

10. I would sing that Brahman and join His Feet!

You make, guard and end all the things, You are the oldest one among the Gods in the spacious heavenly region. You are the first who stands as the endless source. Oh Brahman, You made me Yours, My Lord! When shall I sing and worship You thus and reach Your pair of flower-like feet and dwell in mystic wedlock with You, my perfect Gem?

28. Vazhappatthu (The Ten Hymns of Disgust with Life)

1. To whom else can I appeal against You!

Our Lord! You expanded from earth to heaven, You exist and fill everywhere. You shine in all glory. Look, I have no support but You, Oh King of Shivapuram! Shiva who dwells in sacred Perunthurai, if You who made me Yours should deny me Your grace, then to whom shall I complain and who shall I blame? Look, I cannot bear this life on earth surrounded by Sea. In Your mercy, call me to come to You!

2. You are unknown to gods!

Oh! Supreme Guru, the gem, You made my wretched self Your slave. Look, I have no other support except Your self. The gods themselves do not know of Your unique form. You elude the minds of both. Oh Lord of red-hue, You are Shivapuram's King. You are Shiva who resides in sacred Perunthurai! You are the One supreme Lord who rules over me. In grace, do command me to come to You.

3. I would rejoice with You and quarrel too!

Look, I have no other support except Your Feet which

Vishnu praises and sings of! The King of Shivapuram sought me and made me His, Shiva, You dwell in sacred Perunthurai. I would shrink from You alone and would rejoice with You alone. With You alone would I plead for my safety. I languish for I cannot bear this life here. In grace, do command me to come to You!

4. You burnt the triple forts!

You quickly burnt the forts of the strong giants. Take note, I have no other support except You. The dancer of Thillai is the King of Shivapuram. Shiva, You dwell in sacred Perunthurai. On the day when both of them pierced through the bounds of all the three worlds and saw You, You capably grew without top or bottom. In grace, do command me to come to You, for I cannot bear life here.

5. I have found Oneness with You!

You are the partner of the maid whose words are sweet like nectar. Look, I have no support except You, King of Shivapuram. You made me Yours for certain. Shiva, You dwell in sacred Perunthurai. My thought, my body, my mouth, nose, ears and eyes—all have found unison and oneness with You. I, Your slave, can no longer suffer this life on earth. In grace, call me to come to You.

6. I am a guileful wretch!

You are the partner of Her who has the softest feather-like feet. Look, I have no other support except You. King of Shivapuram, You made me Yours in a fitting manner. You are the Lord Shiva who dwells in sacred Perunthurai. I do fear, making me the cur-like Your own, You gave me grace which my deceitful self forgot due to my ignorance. I cannot live here anymore. In grace, command me to come to You.

7. I am a dark-souled one!

You are the effulgent light like the blessed Sun. Look, I have no support except Your Feet. You are Shivapuram's King of sacred, glorious beauty. You are Lord Shiva, who dwells in sacred Perunthurai. With a melting heart, I see Your mercy. Yet, my dark self does not know how to mix with You, Look at me! I cannot suffer life upon this earth. In grace, do command me to come to You.

8. You are limitless ambrosia!

You are the partner of Her who has fingers of softness like the ball. Behold! I have no support except You. You are the King of holy Shivapuram, who resembles red fire. You are Shiva who dwells in sacred Perunthurai, You are the endless nectar, Rare and Great essence and the rarest ambrosia. You came and made me Your own and gave me salvation. I cannot suffer this life. In grace, do command me to come to You.

9. You shot through the three-fold worlds!

You are the greatest destroyer of sins. Behold, I have no support except You. Oh King of Shivapuram, You are the God of all the gods. You are Lord Shiva in sacred Perunthurai, while Brahman and Vishnu went piercing up and down through the three worlds. You shot up as a roaring flame. You wear the tusker's skin. I cannot any more suffer life. In grace, do command me to come to You.

10. I will praise and worship none but You!

You are the partner of Her whose face is pure and ancient. Behold, I have no support except You. Oh King of Shivapuram, You wear the lovely moon. You are Lord Shiva who dwells in sacred Perunthurai. I will not worship others

or praise or think of them as my support at all. Speak You,
Lord of Buxom bull, I cannot bear to live. In grace, do command me to come to You.

29. Arulppatthu
(The Ten Hymns of Divine Grace)

1. Lord Shiva's glory!

You are the Mighty Jyothi, You are splendour, You are the bright effulgent light. You are the partner of the maid of ambient locks and beautiful breasts. You are the Lord wearing milk-white ashes. You are law unknown to the flower-borne Brahman and Vishnu, You are the first beneath the Kuruntham tree full of flowers in the blessed town of Perunthurai. If I in love call You, do come to me in grace and ask me why I called You?

2. His Omniscience!

Oh! Your dance, the spotless one, the One smeared with ashes. You, the brow-eyed, are the Lord of the heavenly hosts. You are the only one. I searched for You in all the worlds, wailing and raving; but could not see You. You are the essence beneath the Kuruntham tree with fresh flowers in sacred Perunthurai of Supreme tank. If I, in love, call You, do come to me in grace and ask me why I called You?

3. You are the Chief-executive!

Our Chief! You are the leader of my soul. You are the spouse of two good dancers of fragrant locks. You are the fire-eyed Lord who stared at the handsome body of good Kaaman from which a flame rose. You are the fair-eyed beneath the Kuruntham tree with fresh flowers in the midst of sacred Perunthurai. If I call in love, come to me in grace and ask me why I called You?

4. Shiva, the mighty flame!

The four-faced Lotus God, Brahman and the Cloud-hued Kannan could not reach You, the flawless One. Oh Father! when they begged You to disclose Yourself, You rose as a mighty flame. You are the pure one beneath the Kuruntham tree with fresh flowers in Perunthurai of the self-proclaiming Vedas. If I in love call You, do come in grace and ask, Why I called You?

5. Shiva, the sacred saint!

The bosom of Your ash-worn form of fire bears two lustrous, dot-like scars. They were caused by Your own contact with the breasts of Your spouse of curly locks and twin waists. You are the saint beneath the Kuruntham tree of fresh flowers of Perunthurai surrounded by thick groves which are sky high. If I in love call You, come to me and ask me why I called You?

6. Shiva, the rare brilliance!

Pure One! You are of coral colour with pure white ashes smeared on You, You shine with the rare brilliance of diamonds, You give ambrosia which is of intense sweetness to those who think of You within their hearts. You are the master of us beneath the Kuruntham tree of fresh flowers in the rich and sacred Perunthurai.

7. Shiva, the Universal Truth!

You, the utmost truth! You are of changing forms. By bending the bow of Meru mountain with Your mighty hands, You burnt the triple forts of the enemies. You kicked the God of death, dead. You are the Lord of red form like a column of the fiercest flame. You are the Great One beneath the Kuruntham tree with fresh flowers in the rich and sacred Perunthurai. If I in love call You, come to me and ask me why I called You?

8. Abode of bliss!

You, the rare free one! You are the first one. And You are the three-eyed sage, You are the Siddha who granted in grace the great "Abode of bliss" to Your worshippers who worship You with flower buds, who sing of You and pray to You and who think of You in love, You are the Father beneath the Kuruntham tree with fresh flowers in the rich and sacred Perunthurai! If I in love call You, come to me in grace and ask me why I called You?

9. Shiva's Characteristics!

You eyed my darkest soul and drove all my illusions away. You killed all my births in this birth in this world and in the next too. You are the true being. You are the purest one, with braid of red colour, upon which the hissing snake and the Ganges live. You are the grace beneath the Kuruntham tree with fresh flowers in Perunthurai of four luminous Vedas. If I in love call You, come in grace and ask me why I called You?

10. Pray to show the way to His abode!

You dwell beneath the Kuruntham tree with fresh flowers in the sacred Perunthurai surrounded with groves which are fertile and stately. With pangs of heart, I recall that glory, and thinking of You, I pine. If I in love call You as my Lord, then speak Oh! rare sage to me in grace and tell me to come out from this Sea of billows—the world filled with miseries. Also ask me to come to You in the proper way. Also show me the way and tell me that this is the proper way to Holy Kailash!

30. Thirukkazhukkun-drappathigham (The Hymns of Sacred Eagle Mount)

1. Your name is Bliss!

You are the Mighty Lord of peaceful Perunthurai. You are unequalled bliss to those who speak Your name. You are my Lord who wiped all the griefs that came my way. When my deeds both good and evil were viewed alike with equipoise, so that the fertile seeds should not sprout in future. You came and showed Your sacred, unmeasured beautiful form upon the Kazhukkundram.

2. My wayward self!

You are the mighty Madman of Perunthurai, who carried earth for sweet pudding as Your wage. My guilty self which did not follow Your will has not at all so far approached You. You, the best one, are the King of Shivaloka. You came to make my hard heart and grieving self that is baser than a mean cur, Your servant and showed Yourself upon Kazhukkundram.

3. Shiva, the killer of bonds!

In Perunthurai, You had wiped off the tears from the pair of eyes of my own bewildered self. And also You had killed my old bonds which were very strong. Now, I have parted from Perunthurai and am ruined by my sins. I do not know what my future is! I was quite perplexed for I knew not where to place Your pair of glittering Feet which are of red colour. But You came and saved my wild fears and showed Yourself upon Kazhukkundram.

4. You manifest Yourself only to devotees!

Your devotee who is filled with love which is too rare to have, dwells in You and daily worships You. But I was too full of shame that is also rare in man and was sunk in the midst of the Sea of births. But when I had caught hold of and stowed the boat of Perunthurai which is too hard to praise, You showed upon Kazhukkundram, Your sacred form of beauty which is too rare for sight.

5. You are the Time!

You were a sow of quite attractive form, You are the cloud of perfect good of Perunthurai. You are the King of gems, who lodged well within my heart which has no virtues. With all the world as witness, I loved and loved You till You came. And when I worshipped, You came as Time itself and showed Your good self upon Kazhukkundram.

6. You are my consoler!

Oh! Mighty flood of Perunthurai! You gave me constant love that knows no change. In those days, when strangers spoke too ill of me, what had You done for me in their presence? Your pair of Feet which rid death and the death of evils, are my unique refuge. Thus, when I worshipped You in Pure love, You came and showed Yourself upon Kazhukkundram!

7. Shiva, the Generous One!

Oh! Esa, You gave eight qualities to the sixty-four giant maidens. I sank within the sinful fruits of 'dirt' that is triple, strong and old and delusive. But You drove my weariness and made myself Your own and gave me Your pure flower Feet. And tiring me, You came before Your saints and showed Yourself upon Kazhukkundram.

31. Kandappatthu (The Ten Hymns of Darshan—Holiest!)

1. Shiva, the Endless Rapture!

My sense-organs produced illusions in my mind. So, I had been ripe enough to die and roam in higher realms and fall in rare, dark hells. But He purified my heart and made me His and 'Shivam' itself. I saw Him that endless rapture in the beautiful shrine of Holy Thillai.

2. My shameful forgetfulness!

Gripped by griefs and afflictions of births of two-fold, that is, good and evil 'deeds', I was lying worn out without the least thought of You. But I saw You, the peerless one who snapped away my births, and richly made me Your own, worshipped by all the worlds in the Court of Thillai.

3. Shiva, the unseen Guest!

Even when I had not seen Him, He entered my body and stayed in my heart. He made me sublime and He, with mercy, made my soul His own. In the beautiful shrine of Thillai, I, a dog-like slave, saw Him whose delicious abode of bliss is the shrine of Thuruthi with love.

4. Me, a dog, He has blessed!

I had been a base, unlettered dog of mean intelligence. He came as colossal Lord and snapped away the bonds of my soul and gave me His blessings for all to see. I saw Him being worshipped by all in the Court of Thillai.

5. He destroyed my ignorance!

I was tossed about in the whirls of castes, descents and births. He made such a helpless dog-like me His servant and rid me of griefs. He rid me of my ignorance and my notions too of egoism such as 'I' and 'mine'. I saw that flawless ambrosia in the crowded shrine of Thillai.

6. Shiva, the source of the worlds!

In order to kill all my births, from root to branches, to be rid of both illness and old age and sever the bond of kinsmen too, I went and saw that only source of the worlds, worshipped by all sages and gods within the sacred court of Thillai town which is surrounded by groves.

7. He works upon me ceaselessly!

In grace, He cut off the bonds of my own soul which had neither love nor virtue, and thus He made me known as mad. He had bound His Feet by my mental chord, lest I should make Him part from me. I saw the dance of that Omniscient in the Bright Thillai.

8. Guileless gods love Him too!

In ignorance, and in vain, I had been immersed forever here in the depths of countless concepts, I have not known my future. But He, the Endless rapture, condescended and made me His. I saw Him in Thillai worshipped by the guileless gods.

9. Shiva kindled the Light in my heart!

My dog-like life did not know of virtue nor of good conduct. But He caused the Light in my heart to grow and soar, and snapped away my sins and bonds and gave me deathless love and Supreme Grace. I saw Him in the Court of Thillai where the four Vedas flourish!

10. Shiva's diversity!

He is the five elements, He is the five senses and the true essence. He is so great that He is all diversity and yet nothing of these. He is the lustrous light that drove my griefs and made me His. I saw that emerald in Bright Thillai praised by the four Vedas.

32. Prarthanaippatthu (The Ten Hymns of Petitioning)

1. Bliss replaced by weariness!

I was living rapt in silent bliss in the midst of Your saints that day. But those good times have fled away and instead days of woes have dawned on me. So, I am dry and actionless. My Lord! I have grown weary, for I went in search of Your own Light of endless joy. In Your grace, do grant me that I, Your slave, love You.

2. I age in vain!

Some saints have gained Your grace by means of their growing love for You. But I, Your slave, by means of my passions age in vain. I have not yet destroyed this sinking body of mine. My Lord! rid my cruel self of my harsh sins. With Your overflowing sea of grace, grant that I, Your slave, ceaselessly melt in heart for You.

3. Give me true love!

While all Your saints have gone and have plunged within Your wide ambrosial sea of grace, I died wearied here bearing this dark sinful body. My Lord! Oh King of fear that those who see me here should say in dread that I, a mad of the darkest heart, has come, then You grant me in Your grace that true love for You.

4. Give me motiveless love!

You had love for me and in Your grace made me Yours in the midst of Your saints who love and beg of You. Oh! rare ambrosia, Great Gem of Pearl, You resemble the light of the lamp that is quenchless. I wonder if I, Your slave, can be blessed with Supreme love which neither heeds nor begs for anything.

5. 'I' and 'Mine' should go!

Hah! Partner of the spouse of blue and fish-like eyes will Your mercy grant me who is sinful that grace to live in truth in the midst of Your living saints and reach the ancient Supreme Sea of rapture and be rid of the bonds of the soul and the body and egoistic thought of 'I' and 'Mine' and all.

6. Give me infinite Love!

Your saints' hearts melt unceasingly quite free from bondage, while I, a vile dog, wait and wallow away from them, My Lord! so grant me true love, You, the mighty Sea of bliss which does not know shifting, hiding, parting, forgetting, remembering and the measure or end.

7. Cut off my darkness!

While all who say about and saw Your Sea of rapture have avidly consumed it, is it just that I Your slave dog should lie in grief with scourging ills. I forgot to tell You to grant Your grace Yourself to me but left You. My Light, My Lord from now on cut off my darkness with Your own splendorous grace.

8. Hurry to grace me!

Though entering in the midst of Your well-tried saints of melting hearts and growing grace, I stand with mind like a stern bamboosa and I wear off. Oh! Lord Shiva, grant me too that love which Your own saints of beauty have for You. Haste and come with mellowed grace and grant Your golden tender Feet.

9. Grant me ceaseless bliss!

All Your saints attached to You enjoy with pride and in full all Your gifts, You have granted without holding back anything. Shall I, Your slave, weary like strangers? Great Lord of Shivaloka who improved my thoughts by Your glorious grace and made me Your own, do grant me ceaseless bliss which is rapturous.

10. A gourd unbored!

Hah! You are the partner of the fawn-like spouse. You are delicious fruit to Your worshippers. Oh Nambi! say what there is for You if I of unmelting heart were like an unbored gourd. When will the day dawn for me who is cruel to know You who has entered my flesh and when I am graced with a melting heart.

11. Shall I droop distressed?

While all Your saints meet in batches and bend and dance and enjoy bliss, shall I the forlorn and distressed live like a barren tree? My Lord! May it be granted that I should come closer to You and mix with You with a melting heart and dancing body and be bliss itself fixed in You.

33. Kuzhaitthappatthu (The Ten Hymns of Self-Surrender)

1. I, Your slave, surrender!

When the scourge of age-old cruel deeds crushes me, Oh! You are the One, who owns me and protects me. Is it certain that good accrues if I of cruel deeds should labour hard? Lord of Umadevi! make me Yours! Should You not forgive me if I had sinned? It is quite just if I should call and address You as the Lord of braid adorned with the moon. Oh Great Father! Could You withhold Your grace from me who is Your slave?

2. Bid me to serve You!

I had consoled myself well that You had already rid me of all my sorrows and made me Your own. King and Partner of the spouse whose waist is like a creeper. Our own Lord of Shivaloka, speak now, Why did You not welcome me in grace asking me to come and then destroy my body full of ills and pains. Oh Lord! is it enough if You should only chastise me? Should You not call me and make me serve You?

3. My sins as mighty as the Mountain!

That grace of Yours which once saved me and made even me Your own, who is like a vile dog with worth nothing. Has that same grace quite left You and gone away today? You are the partner of Umadevi and the Lord of Myself too. What is the harm that will accrue if You should accept as acts of great virtue even those blunders of mine which are as mighty as the Mountain. Hah! Father of eight shoulders and triple eyes, pity me.

4. Do what You will to me!

Hah! You are the bridegroom of the maid of fawn-like eyes. Oh King! You made me forget all Your glories and You pushed me and made me enter within this fleshy body and caused me to whirl and rot too within it. Yet, You shall Yourself know well the ignorance of me who is Your slave and bless me. Oh King! when will the day dawn when You shall do like this? When will I be called to You and when can I praise You?

5. Shiva's mysterious ways!

You are the tongue itself which speaks of You. You are the organs too from the mouth onwards. You are the way to comfort and You are despair too. You are all the evil and You are all the good too. When Your truthful nature is explained then it will be seen well that nothing else exists. You, of Shivaloka, what is the way to get consoled? Should You not comfort myself when I drown in despair?

6. You are the cause of my desires!

You alone know whatever I must desire here? You grant to me all the things that I so desire. You are rare for Brahman and Vishnu who desire You. You desired me and claimed my service too. I desire only that which You Yourself desire, whatever may be the object and give it to me in grace. Should there be anything else which I may otherwise desire too, is that desire too caused by Your own Supreme Will?

7. Shiva works in mysterious ways!

Did You not on that day itself, when You made me Your own slave, accept my soul, my body and all things as well that had been owned by me as Your own things. You are the Lord of eight shoulders and triple eyes, You resemble a mountain. Pray to tell me if there could ever be even a single hindrance here at all for me. Through me You do right and wrong. I am not the master who could have any say in all these matters.

8. My total surrender to Shiva!

It was You, who desired and made even me, meaner than the meanest of dogs, Your own. I am not vested with the right to weigh and judge anything at all. Except that I should simply place my Maya-generated birth in Your own charge and live silently. How could such authority belong to me here? Oh Lord of eyes of Your brow, may You lodge my soul within a body or may You place it beneath Your anklet Feet.

9. I meditate on His Feet alone!

You are the Lord of Forehead set with an eye. With my own joyful eyes, I was gazing well at Your pair of anklet Feet. Avoid that I should contemplate on anything except those two self-same Feet alone by day as well as by night. My master does it behove me to think and consider whether I should shuffle off this mortal coil on earth or that I should come and reach Your anklet-feet at all? How funny my serfdom would be if I could weigh everything.

10. Shiva, the Vedic sage!

Having discharged all my duties properly till now, My Lord, I, who am Your dog-like slave, rave and rant. You showed me Your form which is rapturous, resplendent and sacred, that day and made my self Your servant too. You, the ancient one, are the glory itself. You are Youthful and You are the handsome Vedic sage, Ah! my own King, You, in Your grace, have denied me Your mighty abode of bliss and blessings and have thus tortured me.

34. Wuyirunnippatthu (The Ten Hymns of Devoured Soul)

1. He is sung by bards!

You are the partner of the spouse of Umadevi whose form is beautiful. You are the killer of all my old deeds. You do not part from my body. You, the rider on bull, You dwell in the Perunthurai sung by worthy poets. Say when I can enjoy and when exult?

2. He graced dog-like me!

Why am I that I should reach Your Feet? You gave to dog-like me a seat, entered my fleshy body and mixed with my soul and left not my own heart. That honey-braided one lives in Perunthurai and He gave me a boon which is unknown to the gods.

3. He gave me frenzy!

I do not know if I am my own-half nor do I know if it is the day or night. You are beyond all thoughts and words. You have a big and raging bull. You are the sage of lasting, sacred Perunthurai, who is the mighty light which gave me a delicious frenzy. I do not know all Your wiles.

4. He dwells in me!

He, Himself, entered my soul and melting all my pores He made me His own. That Lord of Perunthurai again entered me and He lives within my heart, my eyes and my words. Oh! Speak if there is a killer of sins like Him in this world.

5. May You cling to Him!

Oh! you, the ones who are perishing, if you are all rid of all your bonds would you cling to those proper bonds and reach the blissful goal. You hurry then and mix with those who worship the Feet in ways they have been taught, of that Lord who lives in Perunthurai, which is lasting and full of honey.

6. His pranks with me!

He wiped away the wild bonds that swept me like the waves of the Sea, and entered me and filled Himself in my own body and heart and did not leave me. Our Lord who lives in sacred Perunthurai has played all pranks and wears for His crown of broad braid the shining moon.

7. I want nothing!

I do not want fame, I do not want wealth. I do not want earth and heaven. I do not want births and deaths. I do not want to even touch those who do not want Lord Shiva. I have gone and reached the Feet of the Lord of lasting, sacred Perunthurai and have worn them. Hence. I do not want to leave them nor allow them to leave me.

8. He is honey on boughs!

You are our Haran, our rare balm and my King! I cannot suffer any longer, You, spotless Lord of Ash-worn form who dwells in the holy shrine of Perunthurai surrounded with loamy fields. Shall I call You my honey upon the boughs or ambrosia from the roaring Sea.

9. I do not know my future!

Hah me! Our Haran of rarest form is my own ambrosia! He is of form which is the colour of red flower and dwells in sacred Perunthurai, He stands there forever, and He dwells in my heart as my own soul. I know what was past and gone but I do not know what the future holds for me.

10. I stand as a forest tree!

While those in the heavenly world have performed penances, I, in vain, have borne this flesh-packed body and stand as a forest tree. May I ask You who dwell in sacred Perunthurai of honied cassia to grant me Your grace, who is a sinner through and through!

35. Achchappatthu
(The Ten Hymns of Fear)

1. Those who do not love Him!

I fear not either the glistening snakes in the anthills or the strong bodies of the false one, Oh! but how much I would fear, when I see those who would not reach the Feet of that great one of the long braid and forehead eye, but would believe in another god and would not have love for the former.

2. Those who do not scorn lowly gods!

I fear not the destruction that the raging lust brings nor do I fear the Sea of sins. But when I see those who praise other lowly gods and have scorn for our King's own sacred form that is Lord Shiva and cry that He is a lowly god then I fear greatly about their destruction. For, He is the Lord whom both Vishnu and Brahman could not see.

3. Those who do not drink His grace!

I fear not the javelins that wound the flesh, not even glances of the maids wearing bangles. He looks with grace and melts our bodies. He dances within the sacred court. And who would not drink His sweet grace at all. When I see those loveless who do not praise my unbored Gem, Oh! How much we dread them?

4. Those who do not shed tears!

I do not fear the words of the parrot-tongued maids nor their deceitful smiles. They neither reach the Feet of the sage whose form is smeared with white ashes nor do they shed tears from their eyes; they do not pray or weep with mellowed, melting hearts. When I see those ones who are devoid of love, how much we dread them.

5. Those who do not wear Ashes!

I fear not the diseases that would come. I do not fear the births and deaths. How much I dread when I see those who neither mix with the saints of One who wears the crescent moon, nor praise His rosy Feet which Vishnu could not see by splitting the earth, nor wear white ashes.

6. Those who do not praise Him!

I do not fear burning fires or even fear when all the mountains come rolling down. The shoulders of the Lord of bull shine with white ashes, and He is the master who is beyond all the worlds. How much I dread when I see those ones who do not serve Him with a melting heart and do not praise His Lotus-feet with flowers.

7. Those who do not melt!

I do not fear guilt that is forced upon me nor would I at all fear death. He dances in the shining court swinging His hand which holds the fire. He is the first one who wears wreaths of cassia which are shining. Oh! How much I dread when I see those who would neither praise nor melt at His Feet.

8. Those who do not praise His Feet!

I do not fear tuskers chained to the poles nor do I fear

the fire-eyed tigers. He is our master of sweet and fragrant braided locks. Oh! How I dread when I see those ignorant ones who cannot live with greatness and sweetness and praise His anklet feet unknown to the gods.

9. The false ones!

I do not fear thunderbolts from the clouds nor do I fear the friendship of kings. He is our Lord who ate poison as His food. He is our King who has well made me His own. Oh! How much I dread to see those ones who dread to smear the holy ashes on their heads.

10. The unmanly ones!

I do not fear the murderous arrows nor do I fear the wrath of Yama (God of death) Himself. When I see milk-sops, I dread them much for they would not think of the Lord of the baby moon in their hearts which should thrill and melt. And they would not with tearful eyes stand and praise and worship Him.

36. Thiruppandip-pathigham (The Sacred Pandi Hymns)

1. I know none but Him!

I offer worship at the anklet-feet of the partner of the mountain's daughter. He is the rare ambrosia of Pandians too. He is One and not anyone. He is the warrior on the steed who had shown His own self and melted. My heart knows no other form except His own.

2. He comes on horse to give God-mania!

We proclaim that those who reach Him will drop their ego and become God-manias. Learn that when that Light which eclipsed the Sun comes on horseback holding Trishul in hand, all births and life would at once fly away; it will drive off and prevent future births of the King of Madurai.

3. The four floods!

That One came riding a horse to give a flood of joy to the world. He captured the hearts of His devotees with His own form of delightful flood. You, men who would like to swim and bathe in the delightful flood of water, and to taste His anklet-feet in the flood of rapture which is great.

4. He would slash our births!

You, good ones do not seek the clustering births, of all ages, this is the age when the Lord of good Pandiland rules and shines. He rides a horse of great rapture and handling the bright, unsheathed sword of spiritual knowledge and mysteries, He would slash all opposing births and roll them down.

5. He distributes His treasure grace!

When there is time enough pray and make love to Him to save Yourselves, He is that rare one who ate poison and whom the "Creator of the Earth", Brahman and the gods could not reach. Hurry you and reach Him, for just now the Lord of Pandiland distributes His treasures which is salvation, to His own saints.

6. He prize of great release!

Even the Pandyan could not notice and speak of the equestrian light which drove the thick darkness of illusions and illumined all the things. Even while you won't strive and live at His Feet, there is no bar. This is the prize of great release the Lord of Pandi bestows.

7. He is of bounteous boons!

The moment He comes on the fine but false horse and takes charge of you, all foes of birth will fly away and die. He grants His grace of rare and great glory to His own wards to give them bliss. Hence, you reach the rosy Feet of Tennan of plentiful boons.

8. He would gift away all the worlds!

He who lives and is endless soaked in the flood of rapture, showed us His changeless mercy, killed all our cruel deeds and rooted out our age-old bond and made us His. Hurry you and reach the Feet of that Great Pandiland Lord who would gift away all the worlds.

9. The beautiful maids lost themselves!

He is the Lord of Pandi, who melts the bones of all those saints who pray that they should cross the Sea of future births and clinging deeds. The fragile beauties who caught sight of Him on the horse lost their hearts to Him and all became wooden and they forgot their own selves too.

10. Cleave to His conquering Feet!

He conquered the God of death and the five senses and with His powerful spouse, He sat in state beside the Pandyan King. All you doubting souls reach Him and firmly cling to His Feet. He is the Mighty Knight who crushed the lives of all the foes.

37. Pidhitthappatthu (The Ten Hymns of Devout Grip)

1. Mystic union of Universal fullness!

Oh! You are the King of the heavenly ones. You are the mystic union of Universal fullness. You mellowed my foul-minded self and made my whole stock Your own, and gave me bliss which transcends all life. Oh! You are the Balm and the clearest end of everything which has end. You are of glorious foot, my wealth of grace and You are my Lord Shiva. I hold You firmly within my grip for our sake. How can You in grace henceforth give me the slip?

2. I lie prostrate!

You are the King of the Heavenly hosts; You are pleased with the eternal bull. You are the true essence of my sinful self. Oh My God! You are the Ocean of great mercy. You saved me and made me Yours, lest I, Your slave, should lie prostrate like miasmic mud within my body which has grown foul with worms. I continuously hold You firmly within my grip. So, how can You, in grace, hereafter escape from me?

3. Ambrosia mellowed out of love!

You are my mother and father and Oh! You are the peer-less one, Gem. You are the rare ambrosia which is mellowed out of love, You dispensed well the best and purest bliss of Shiva to my mean and wandering self of a rotten body which multiplies falsehood but shortens the time for doing good things. Oh! You are my Supreme Wealth and You are my Lord Shiva. I hold You firmly within my grip in this life itself. So, how can You, in grace, hereafter escape from me?

4. Resplendence of rare concentration!

You are the splendorous light of grace. You are the juice of mellowed fruit. You are the King of rare ascetics of mighty grace. You are the truth of all arts. You are the enjoyment beyond all praise. You are the resplendence of rare concentration. You entered the hearts of saints of clear vision. You are my supreme wealth. You are my Lord Shiva. In the midst of the darkness, I hold You very firmly in my grip. So, how can You, in grace, hereafter escape from me?

5. You are the help in my weariness!

You are the one without comparison. You are the shining light that illumines the mind of my self who is Your own slave. To my worthless self which does not know the proper goal, Oh My Love! You, in grace, dispense the best of bliss. Oh! God of lovely splendorous light, no one can describe You. You are my supreme wealth, You are my Lord Shiva. In my weariness, I hold You firmly within my grip. So, how can You, in grace, hereafter escape from me?

6. Our great possession!

Oh! Pingnakan, You are our Mighty possession. You dwell in my driest heart, as if it were Your shrine. You made me Yours too by bestowing rapture which is boundless. You rooted out all births and claimed all my line of ancestry as Your own. You are the rarest vision seen in space by me, Your slave. Oh! You are my Supreme wealth. Oh! You are my Lord Shiva. Even in death, I hold You firmly within my grip. So, how can You, in grace, hereafter escape from me?

7. God of superb splendour!

You are the age-long one who cut off the roots of all my births and in Your grace taught me the way to cling to You. You were pleased with my worship and so You entered my own heart too and showered on me Your pair of bejewelled Feet. You are the Resplendent Light and Oh! God of Superb Splendour, You are my wealth and Oh! You are my Lord Shiva. Oh Esa! I hold You very firmly within my grip, so how can You, in grace, hereafter escape from me?

8. You blossomed out as all lives!

Oh Father! You are the first one who expanded and stood from earth to heaven. You are endless and the wonderfully-powered great one. Your own saints have held You in their grip. Oh My Supreme wealth, You are My Lord Shiva, Oh You Esan, you blossomed out as all the lives and yet parted from them and stood out as a distinct one, Oh You! Trickster, I hold You firmly within my grip. So, how can You, in grace, hereafter escape from me?

9. You are dearer than a Mother!

You have in Your grace with more love and tenderness than that of a mother who instinctively feeds her baby at her breasts, melted the heart of my own sinful self, Your slave and made my inward light glow with great lustre. You poured out in me a ceaseless stream of honey which is rapturous and also roamed along with me. Oh! You are supreme wealth, Oh! You are my Lord Shiva. Even in my pursuit, I hold You firmly within my grip. So, how can You, in grace, hereafter escape from me?

10. My body is His golden shrine!

Oh! Pure and flawless Gem, You are Esa! You entered my body of meanest flesh and made it Your grand and golden shrine. You softened every pore, melted every bone and quite easily You made me Your own. You are the true splendour. You cut off all bonds like griefs, my births and deaths and all my delusive thoughts too. Oh! You, the bliss, I hold You firmly within my grip. So, how can You, in grace, hereafter escape from me?

38. Thiruvesaravu (The Sacred Grief)

1. Shiva works wonders!

You dragged me of iron heart very often and melted my bones and gave me the sweet-cane taste of Your bejewelled Feet. You are the one of braided locks wherein the billowing Ganga flows. You turned all jackals into mighty steeds. That is Your Supreme Grace!

2. The Goal is reached!

You are the partner of the spouse of music words. To Your slaves, You are rare nectar for them to feast upon. My Lord! You made me Yours and cut away my earthly births. I served at Your Feet, since You called me to come, and feasted my eyes. Thus I reached my goal!

3. Shiva came to my help!

I was helpless without the help of relations and so I was inclined to sink within the rare hells of births and deaths. But You, my master who ate poison from the roaring Sea, pitied me, Your slave. Oh You, greatest Lord! How well You had disclosed Your flower-like Feet!

4. You saved my soul!

Oh You, of long flowing braid, You sported and played with green-tongued snakes. You are the Lord of those who have Your feet as their crowns. You saved me, a slave, from praising the petty gods of the weaker souled ones. Ah me, how wonderful it is that at the very thought of Your glory itself my soul is saved!

5. Shiva ranked my high!

I have not learnt the wisdom of any arts, nor would my heart melt too. and yet, I know not any other God except You of mystic word. I reached Your Feet and lived exultantly. Our Lord, is not the gift of Your gold-grace to me, Your slave, like an offering of a golden-seat to a dog?

6. Shiva destroyed my lust!

I was afflicted by the side-glances of the soft-footed maids. I trembled due to the griefs which mounted like poison. But I was, Oh My Lord and King, saved by Your own grace. And You well blessed me, Your slave and told me not to fear. So, fine You are! the ambrosia of the Thillai court!

7. Your very glance redeems!

Here in this world, You wiped away my desert-like births, Lord Shiva. You dwell in sacred South Perunthurai which is unknown to the gods. Oh Lord! in grace, You entered my heart with love and melted it and made me Yours by casting a graceful glance at me!

8. Shiva is Timeless!

You are the ancient one. You are the first one who does not turn old. You are the true essence of the endless Vedas. You bloomed and flowered as those who are and those who are not. By Your mercy, You again entered my swirling self and made me Yours. How fine it is my Lord?

9. Your mercy knows no bounds!

Oh! My father, living in Idaimaruthur, bless me that Your Foot which like a flower that is sweet for higging grows within my heart, that with a melting heart, I rave about in every street and praise You as Lord Shiva and that I plunge into Your wide Sea of mercy which I have already tasted!

10. Holy 'Shivayanama' gives Liberation!

I have not done any penance except uttering 'SHIVAYANAMA'. Lord Shiva who tastes as honey and sweet ambrosia, Himself came and entered my heart. He so blessed me, His slave, and that day itself I loathed this tortured life of the body.

39. Thiruppulambal
(The Sacred Lament)

1. I praise nothing except Your Feet!

You who are unknown to the Lotus-Brahman and Vishnu. You are the partner of the spouse with sharp breasts and which are adorned with kongu flowers. You, the white-ashed One, You own Arur which is surrounded with lofty walls. I, Your salve, will praise nothing else except Your beautiful Feet!

2. I know no other help except You!

You, of braided locks, You swing the fire, Your weapon is the glittering Trishul! You, Supreme Light, are the Lord of the flock of souls. You own the buxom white bull and Perunthurai which is surrounded with groves. My master! I do not know of a mightier help for me except You!

3. I want a melting heart!

I do not want friends and relations, I do not want a town nor do I want a name, I do not want learned men. My own learning too will hereafter be enough. Oh You dancer! dwelling in Kuttralam! I want a heart that thrills and melts for Your own anklet-feet, just as a cow's heart melts for its calf!

40. Kulappatthu
(The Ten Hymns of
Divine Thillai)

1. He alone is to be sought!

I thought the potsherd and the kaupia as my sole aids and was sure that what is to be sought with a melting heart is the Foot of Shiva alone. I, a slave who dances while all my body and soul too dances, have clung to the Lord and Ruler who dances in bright Thillai (Chidambaram).

2. I will not be reborn!

Though urged by the lust for the shoulders of the maids who have slender waists and speak sweet words and though I would perform sinful deeds in plenty, I will not die, nor will I be reborn again, since I, His slave who has been laid at His twin Feet, have reached the Lord of Bright Thillai.

3. My senses of pairs purified!

He melted all the bones of my body and killed my mighty twin deeds. He wiped away all my griefs and made my sense of pairs also guile pure. He rooted out all age-old bonds too and then He in love entered me. I have reached that Supreme Lord who rules in Bright Thillai.

4. He is the nectar in graceful hearts!

The ones of pure souls will find it hard to part from Him, for they separate themselves from those who do neither know any signs or goals, nor ways or any virtues. I have reached that Lord of shining Thillai where the bliss of Shiva, which springs like nectar in graceful hearts, is known.

5. The consummation attained!

All those saints have reached the right grace and dwell and drink of the honey of Lord Shiva's grace, for they had closed the crater of their births and saved themselves from the flaws of 'Name' and 'Quality' which had bound them. By following the same way, I too reached the King of Bright Thillai.

6. My mind trusts Him!

For fear, my body should drop down dead here like a bud on the branch which grows at first as a flower and then too soon into a ripe and mellowed fruit and then drop. My mind trusts in Him alone. To make my mind approach Him, I approach Thillai of the most beautiful gold and I have reached its Lord.

7. His Feet planted on me!

I rejoice in triumph that I have no more bonds, because the self-same Feet which crushed the mighty shoulders of the famous valiant giants, rest upon my head. And I go there and have thus reached the Lord of Bright Thillai.

8. The pranks of the senses will go!

The wildest pranks of my five senses of overwhelming strength will be wiped off, since His sacred Feet which followed the black and wildest boar which dug down in the forest, have been planted on my head and since I have reached the Lord of Bright Thillai.

9. I tumbled upon a treasure!

I was lying like the barren soil which produces no yield. Yet through my past penances of previous births, I tumbled upon a treasure-trove. To serve that Saivism with my mean head I have reached the Lord of the ruddy Lotus-feet, in this Shining Thillai.

10. No more life on earth!

His partner is like a tender bough, with striped and heaving breasts. With my righteous mind, I do His sacred service. And He will wipe off the entire fruits of my service, which accrue in this life. I have reached Him who is the Master and Lord of Shining Thillai.

41. Arbhuthappatthu (The Ten Hymns of Miracle)

1. He showed His form!

I was infatuous and was caught within the Ocean of life in this world. I fell within the whirls of the dainty maids and got confused. But He prevented me and gave me His own sacred grace to leave all this falsehood. He showed me His pair of Feet and stood disclosing His truest form to me. I cannot describe this great miracle!

2. He gave the mighty grace!

I did not ceaselessly shower flowers and worship Him forever in this manner. So, I got entangled within the meshes of the maids of scented breasts and so had my head turned off. For fear, I should enter grief, He came and gave me grace. He showed His jewelled Feet and stood like King in space in front of me. I cannot describe this great miracle!

3. With repeated blows He fed me with sweet!

I pretended, acted and spoke all lies, upon this earth. The illusions of egoism of 'I' and 'mine' bit me. Sins issued forth from the gash of such wounds thus caused and so I raved and wandered everywhere. But, He, the rarest King who is sought after by the great Vedas, caught hold of me, His slave, and stood in front of me. He gave me repeated blows and made me taste the sweetest things. How can I describe this great miracle?

4. He came with His spouse!

Giving no thought to the births and deaths that come, I did not speak truth, but went on telling lies alone. I was assailed by the eyes of the dark-haired maids and so I lay wallowing, prostrate and bewildered. But with the anklets of His beautiful red Feet tinkling, He came with His beautiful spouse. And as precious help, He made me His and blessed me. How can I know of this great miracle?

5. He gave me His Feet!

I was intoxicated by wealth and all the rest of the enjoyments. I mixed freely with friends and relatives and worthy maidens. I was assailed by their true natures there. But still I fondled them and went wandering about. Then, He gave me freedom from everything and killed all my evil deeds and showed me His flower-like Feet. He entered my heart, stirred me and made myself His own. I know not this great miracle!

6. Sea of Excellence!

I gave no thought to the cycles of births and deaths that come round and round. But, I twined myself in the embrace of beautiful maidens and had sunk within the great flood of saliva of their mouths, and also wandered and roamed about madly. But without any signs and qualities, He, the Sea of excellence combined with His good spouse, came and made me His and gave me His grace. I do not know this great miracle!

7. He showed me His Feet!

I did not worship Him at His Feet of golden anklets in the manner I should do, by selectively choosing good flowers and showering them and by chanting well the five sacred letters (Namashivaya) without fail, within this fleshy life itself. And I was assailed by the dark eyes of the maids with broad breasts and lay supine. But my father showing His flowery feet came and made me His own and gave me His grace. I know not this great miracle!

8. He removed my lust!

He completely wiped off both my deeds of good and evil which swing my body this side and that. He cannot be known to those who would only know Him by mere hearsay. But he illuminated me and made me know Him. He cut off the bonds that forever cling to me and by His supreme and great mercy He removed my lust and placed me in the midst of His saints. I know not this great miracle!

9. He has made me His!

I lay distressed in this forest of births, like a dog with head of rotten wounds. I roamed abroad and did the bidding of the beautiful maidens, and thus mated with the wicked. But, He disclosed on this earth to me His anklet Feet which are the fragrant flowers. That Father has thus even made me His and blessed me and I know not this great miracle!

10. He gave me the spiritual knowledge!

Giving no thought to all these births and deaths which come crowding, I thought of deceitful acts and mean tricks and fondled the fish-like eyes of the maidens with luxurious tresses. But the overall Lord and my own King showed me His own limitless pair of flower-like Feet and giving me

knowledge of the spiritual mysteries, He made me His own
with grace, I know not this great miracle!

42. Sennippatthu (The Ten Hymns of the Head)

1. The Triad too could not see Him!

You are the God of gods, the true Hero and the King of south Perunthurai. You are the first one and You are God of rapture whom even the trio could not see. You are the flowering light of splendour whom all except His loving ones do not know. Our heads shall dwell and brightly glow beneath His pure, great flower-like red Feet.

2. The rapture-flood of sweet nectar!

You are the beautiful God of eight-fold form. You are the rapturous flood of sweet nectar. You are the good one, the true King of Shivaloka, the warrior of the south Perunthurai. You are the beautiful one who placed the spouse of fragrant, long locks in Your half. Our heads shall dwell and blossom forth beneath His round great flower-red Feet.

3. He steals bangles of maids!

Oh! You maids, do look at me. He is our Lord who makes us serve the warrior and chief who dwells in Perunthurai surrounded with coco-palm groves. He steals the bangles of beautiful maids. He takes our souls and services too. Our heads shall dwell and glow gleamingly beneath His bright and flowery red Feet.

4. Surrounded by Siddhars, He dances!

You are the great one who came on earth as a sage, surrounded by Your saints. You are Shivapuram who dances surrounded by the siddhars in Old Thillai. Entering our homes like a Trickster, You come and make us serve You. Our heads shall dwell and blossom forth beneath His Great flower-feet which are planted.

5. He showed Himself and said 'Behold'!

He gave me grace so that I should not consider this delusive birth as true. You are the partner of the bright shouldered Umadevi. You are the dweller on Our Perunthurai. Nectar surged and swelled in me when He showed Himself and said 'Look'. Our heads shall dwell and glow gleamingly beneath His Great rosy flower-feet.

6. He placed us beyond three worlds!

He killed all our evil 'deeds'. He entered our hearts and made us His. He gave His saving love with which we picked flowers and placed at His golden Feet. At once, He gave us liberation and placed us all beyond this three-fold world. Our heads shall dwell and blossom forth beneath that master's great flower-red Feet.

7. He placed us amidst saints!

In grace, He showed His great glorious mercy so that we swim through this sea of births. He pitied me who is helpless and placed me in the midst of His gracious band of saints in relation with whom He saved me and made myself His. The saints showed me the might of that King's true nature.

Our heads shall dwell beneath those red Feet and shine brightly.

8. He removes the body's falseness!

He removes the falseness of this body which is transient and which is stuffed with worms. The saints call You the beautiful light. They call You Esa and say that You are their own Lord and their own father. The saints worship with joined palms while their own flower-like eyes rain down tears. Our heads shall dwell and blossom forth beneath those unfailing flower-feet.

9. He makes His saints' bliss grow!

He is of the heaven who calls my self which is vainly roaming and destroys all the foes of my mighty 'deeds'. He is the Lord who pierced this earth and stood even beyond it. His Feet bless His loving ones and make the bliss of His saints to grow profusely. Our hearts shall dwell and glow brightly beneath those great, gold, flower-red Feet.

10. You come to Him to bow down now!

You are the Mukthan, the foremost light, the three-eyed father and the original seed of all things, You are the siddha and the King of Shivaloka. Oh you, devotees who sing His name and roam, come all of you now and bow down to Him, so that He may kill all our bonds. Our heads shall dwell and glow brightly beneath his Red-Feet which are placed in our hearts.

43. Thiruvaarthai
(The Sacred Word)

1. He came on earth!

You are the partner of Umadevi. You are the one experienced in the Vedic word. You are the great splendour in the flower. You are the supreme mercy which is flawless. You make the conduct of Your saints quite good. You are the virtuous Lord of Perunthurai which is filled with flower gardens and thus You disclosed to us that You are the primal deity. Our Lords are those who know that grace.

2. He graced the dame at Idaimaruthur!

You are that Esan who had blessed Brahman, Vishnu and Indhra when they bowed. You descended on earth and disclosed Your perfect ways. You, in Your grace, gave supreme virtues to that good dame of Idaimaruthur that is full of mansions set with good and brightful gems. Our Lords are those who know that grace.

3. He spread His Net!

You are the ancient God and the plaited King of gods. You, the rapturous dancer, made the six-fold sect to worship You. You, the maid-mad one, getting within the boat spread the gem-set nets for fish. You are worshipped by heaven and earth. You, the graceful one of Perunthurai, kill all ills. Our Lords are those who know the way.

4. He rode a sportful steed!

You are the Lord and Shiva in the guise of a woodman who stayed on the mountain of Mahendhra and whom the needy gods came in search of. You saved us slaves who think of You. That day, that master who is the first one of Perunthurai, rode the sportful steed and made friends found everywhere Your own. Our Lords are those who know His nature.

5. He graced Mandodhari of Lanka!

You were like a Sea of Great mercy, when the heavenly ones came and prayed, and You, in grace, broke the old bonds of Your saints. You are the first one of Perunthurai and Our Lord who crossed the Sea of waves that day and blessed the dame with soft fingers, of Lanka surrounded with lofty walls. Our Lords are those who know His nature.

6. He suckled boars as a sow!

You are the bowman who had burnt the three forts. As a hunter, who is surrounded by the hounds, You, My Lord went into the woods and led the gods who performed Your commands. That day, Esan! My Father! the first One of Perunthurai pitied the boars and breast-fed them as a humble sow. Our Lords are those who know this truth.

7. He beamed as Light!

You! Our own Esan, beamed out as light while both the maids dwelling in the lotus flowers of humble bees, praised and bowed and worshipped You, showering flowers. Our pure one of Perunthurai in grace, You came on earth and killed the sense of diversity. Our Lords are those who know this greatness too.

8. He embraced the Sea-King's maids!

Your chest is adorned with the garlands of the Cassia flowers. You are the Hero who killed the sharp-clawed tiger. You are the partner of Umadevi, the King of the south and of Perunthurai which is surrounded by groves. You are my own Esan and Pure fame who embraced the maids of the Sea-king, emerging from the fire. Our Lords are those who know His form.

9. He nipped my grief!

You are our Lord and who smears pure white ashes. You are the splendour King of Mahendhram. You are the Esan who granted Your Feet to be worshipped by gods. You are the Tennan, the King of Perunthurai, who that day with love showed mercy and showed Your Feet too. You melted me and nipped away my griefs and in grace made me Yours. Our Lords are those who know His nature.

10. He stole the maids' bangles!

You, of gracious eyes, are my own Lord and the Lord of all gods. You are the nectar to the saints. You are the Lord of ours who came on earth and killed the bonds and graced me with the bliss of both worlds. You are the all-wise King of Perunthurai, of sandalpaste, who stole the conch-bangles and that day reached Madurai, full of maids. Our Lords are those who know that way.

44. Ennappathigham (Devout Musings)

1. Show Your form!

I want riddance of the cycle of births in this body on the earth. I want devotion too. Oh! Lord Shiva of glorious form, You are my rare ambrosia of rare form resembling the red-lotus flower. Right in the midst of Your band of saints, show Your grace of unique form and accept me in grace and save me.

2. Was Your promise false!

I am not fit to be Your slave! Yet, my dog-like self cannot for a moment endure to live far from You. Our Lord! Was it all false when You in grace said You won't part, You won't. I know not what it is. You are the great one. who showed Your bejewelled Feet in mercy and said 'Behold'!

3. You, swallower of the soul!

Oh! King of my soul, are You shy so as not to grant in grace Your friendship too? You gave me grace to melt my bones and showed Your pair of flower-like Feet and thus made me Yours before. You are my Lord who gives pleasures and melts and swallows my soul. You are the sage who is the source of all sages.

4. I bear not Your separation!

Though I am void of love, though I bowed not then, though I am not love-mad to see Your great Feet and though I do not rave, yet my Lord kill my births. I appealed to You in this way calling You a pearl, a gem and saying You are the first one. I even asked whether it is just and followed You ever so much. Hence, I cannot bear leaving You.

5. I blush to see You again!

I do not anymore see Your sacred Feet and seeing them with gladdened eyes I no more pray to You. My Lord, of late I have ceased to madly rave for You. I have lost even the virtue of melting in thought of You. I have ceased to see You, since I am so mean. Should You come once more, I would blush again even to see You.

6. I would rave and call Him!

You are that Lord adorned with milk-white ash. You are that splendorous light which came in great grace and gave the gracious path to saints who are truthful. Though I am void of good, I would yet hail and think of You as my ambrosia. Also, I would pray, rave, praise and call on You and thus would I satiate my heart. My Lord! speak in grace, and come!

45. Yaatthiraippatthu (The Ten Hymns of Pilgrimage)

1. The commencement of the pilgrimage!

He, the King whose braid is adorned with flowers, is our Lord wearing the snakes too. By mingling in our souls, He would melt the hearts of ourselves who are low. Come with one mind those of you who have been made His own by love and are called by Him to come unto Him by His flood of grace. The time has come to leave the false ones and join the Feet of the master.

2. Leave of sense-world and the rest!

Do not enter the world of the senses. But you ponder much on the Feet of the Lord of snake-jewels. Do not be in want for the rest of the things. Let everything go. He made our dog-like selves His slaves by entering the world which laughed at us. Those who reach the Lord of mercy will not falter or wear out.

3. Be ready to start!

Those saints of His are their own friends and relations.

They have no other. They are their own laws and ways. There is no 'We' and nor 'Ours'. There are no bonds are no illusions. Oh you! devotees leave all these behind and move forward with the Lord's true saints and cherish His sign as your only goal. You be ready to reach Buyangan's Feet by dropping off all the falsehood.

4. He will surely keep us in Shivaloka!

Oh! you who have been made His saints, leave off your sports and worldly games. Come all of you and reach His fragrant Feet and hold on to His sacred will. He will remove this painful body and place us all in Shivaloka. May your minds seek refuge in the flowery Feet of the ash-worn Buyangan, Lord Shiva.

5. Follow the caravan of pilgrim-saints!

Leave off the scourge of wrath and lust. There is not much time to lose. Agree to follow the caravan of the saints in their march to the Feet of the master. May we hurry to Shivapuram and reach there before the gates are closed. Standing beside Him, let us melt and praise the glories of King Buyangan.

6. May we stand before the Shivapuram saints!

All you devotees praise Him and worship Him and adorn Him with flowers. Plant the Feet of Buyangan within your hearts. Despite all griefs, let us all reach the bright, great Shivapuram and bow before the Feet of Lord Shiva, so that no hindrance should come to us hereafter. And in the presence of the gracious saints let us melt in heart and stand and live.

7. Do not tarry in this fleeting world!

Those who want to delay let them do so. Because we

cannot tarry in this fleeting world. Henceforth we rush to the golden Feet of King Buyangan whose form is golden. And all you who stand off, do not delay, but decide on how to stand near Him. If you should lag behind and sleep, it would be hard to gain access to the Lord.

8. Let us enter while the gate is open!

All of you are so blessed that you shall not part from the great bliss of the Lord. Deluded you would later on rave and rant in grief and cry Alas! Even while the Gem-set door of sacred Shivapuram is kept open, let us reach there and join the sacred Feet of Buyangan whom Vishnu does not know of.

9. Prepare your minds to enjoy the bliss!

Keep your minds prepared with the pure thought of joining Him and ponder on the partner of the spouse with dart-like eyes. He is Buyangan, so quench your thirst and plunge within the grace which is like nectar, with stateless love. Leave off wallowing within falsehood and live beneath Shiva's own Feet.

10. Enter the Shivaloka!

Even by rolling, bowing and praising if you are not His today, then later on you will lie confused in the dark and will lose esteem. Hence do this to gain true vision. Besides, who else would gain the grace of Buyangan and the King of Shivaloka, in this wide world.

46. Thiruppadaiezhuchi (The Spiritual Mobilization)

1. The hordes of mighty illusions shall not win!

He is the teacher handling the sword of wisdom. He beats and blasts His Nadam-drum. He is the teacher riding the mighty bull. Hold high His bright Umbrella, the Moon. All of you enter inside the weighty Armour made of holy ash and capture the heavenly city against the hordes of mighty illusions.

2. We will rule heaven!

Oh you, saints! lead the vanguard! All you, devotees move on to the flanks. All you, yogis of shining might lead the main and mighty army. Oh all you, Siddhars of solid strength hold on to the rearguard. The army of ill-luck shall not come near us and all of us will rule Heaven.

47. Thiruvenba (The Sacred Stanzas)

1. My falsehood and two-fold deeds have not gone!

Within my heart, I have not carried the red fire that spits out honey in sacred Perunthurai. Hence, my two-fold hot deeds of good and evil are not burnt and gone away. My body will not melt, nor does my falsehood go to dust. Oh! What shall I do?

2. How shall I praise His dear ones!

Shall I bow and shout in joy or rave or dance? Shall I sing or stare at. Oh! Great Lord, What shall I do before the one who says that You are the one who is of Perunthurai and who charges us with delicious joy.

3. He has darted a javelin in my heart!

I do not know what all faults I have committed and nor do I know the way by which I could be saved by worshipping His rosy Feet. The Lord who dwells in Perunthurai came on earth and stayed here and darted His sharp, unsheathed javelin within my heart.

4. He is the medicine for miseries!

Having wiped off my old deeds of good and evil, He, Tennan, the mighty One will wipe off my future births. He is of infinite mercy and He dwells in Perunthurai. He is the balm that cures all the future woes too.

5. He never leaves my heart!

Both the Vedic creator of all the worlds and Vishnu did not know that He is the Lord and by whom both of them got confused too. The King who dwells in Perunthurai resides within my heart today without parting. I reward those who know this truth.

6. He makes me crazy!

He kills all my births, makes me frenzied and fills my heart also with intense rapture which is beyond all speech. He is my father of Perunthurai who makes me His and views me with mighty grace. Then, He came that ambrosia and deathless, Infinite Bliss.

7. He spreads Light!

The Brilliance which was spread by the One who dwells within my heart and within the sacred, glorious shrine of Perunthurai too, showed me realms from where there is no return. This Brilliance came to me and rested as the changeless, rare ambrosia too.

8. His wonderful condescension!

You are glory which is superior to all glories and You placed me, a slave, who is inferior to all, in mighty bliss. This bliss no one else has known. My Lord! in return for this what is there that I can give You at all.

9. His unparalleled excellence!

He is the Lord who could not be described by all the three, by all the thirty-three and by all the rest of the gods also. But if we praise His Feet which rode upon and trod the earth, then the supreme bliss will fill and swell within the bodies of everyone.

10. Ask and He will give!

He is the One of great mercy and dwells in the Shrine of Perunthurai. He reached my heart in the form of sweet ambrosia, and thus by dwelling there, He made me His own. Oh! my mind, think only on His Feet. Beg of Him and He will grant you all.

11. My heart is His home-town!

He always drove away my darkness and cut off my bonds of griefs. He multiplied my bliss and He planted His good love in the form of lustrous light. That glorious one of Perunthurai delightfully made my heart as His own good home-town.

48. Pandaya Naanmarai (The Ancient Vedas—Four)

1. Is there a return for His grace!

The four ancient Vedas, Brahman and Vishnu could not even approach Him nor could they see Him, Oh My mind! Is there a just return to Him, My God and Kokazhi's Lord who has in grace well made my lowly self His own servant?

2. Worship Him and kill your births!

That bountiful King who rode up the horse of flood formed by the trickling luscious honey has destroyed all the three great bonds. All you of His Perunthurai praise Him. If only you all praised Him, then the root and branch from the jungle of your births will vanish off.

3. His manifold forms!

He is a hunter in the wild forest. He is a fisherman on the Sea; He is a horseman on the land; He who is of Perunthurai's shrine all bless us, rooting out our 'deeds'. Oh! my mind to wipe off your darkness praise His fine Feet which are like the lotus flowers.

4. His worshippers will be saved!

Our kinsmen are they who worship well and pray to Him within the sacred Perunthurai which heavenly ones reach and surround and praise. They alone are the Lords who have lived well and who have their 'deeds' killed off. They deserve the praise of the worlds.

5. Come and see the King of Kokazhi!

We approach Perunthurai to make our griefs fly away. We think and see the lustrous King of Kokazhi who dwells there in the temple of Uttharakosamangai where He does not part but dwells with His own sweet-tongued spouse.

6. Praise the Lord of Perunthurai!

Oh Mind! Speak endlessly of that One who would never depart from Perunthurai and who is the Great one seen and worshipped well by saints who cherish their sense-organs as charged with divine bliss. And by all who would be too glad to be rid of their old chain of births.

7. I wipe my birth with the word 'Perunthurai'!

You are the aim and the end of all the truths, that are much honoured by the world. By singing with gem-like words upon that flawless gem that is beyond words and with having His own Feet as good balm held within my heart, I have cut off all my births by crying 'Perunthurai'!

49. Thiruppadaiaatchi (The Spiritual Exploits of the Sacred Hordes)

1. Lord Shiva's exploits!

My twin eyes shall see His jewelled Feet in joy; my own life shall not be worse than that of damsels copy; we shall forget the ways of being born on earth, we shall worship the pair of Feet unknown to Vishnu, we shall perform dance and sing the mirthful tunes, we shall sing the exploits of the King of good Pandi, we shall disclose the mystic changes loved by heaven. The woodman casting His net for fish should disclose Himself.

2. Tasting the Lord!

We shall cease mixing one with one and five with five; we shall live as the servants of His own saints; we shall move like the cows that start in thoughts of the calf. No sourceless, causal qualities will fill our thoughts. The trembling doubts of good and evil will fly off! We shall all approach the saints and follow them. We shall ever enjoy the overfilled ambrosia. The Lord of Bull and the Iing of myself should enter me.

3. Shiva fills my soul!

The perverse nature of the bonds shall fly away, ambrosia shall spring high in the hearts of fancy, the endless whole shall be caught within our soul, the first and great Supreme Light shall show itself; the sorrows caused by the red-lipped maidens shall die. The fish-like eyes shall enjoy His sacred form; the woes of life shall leave off. Esan! My own Lord should confront me with His sacred form.

4. The Lord's visit!

My jewelled breasts shall enjoy His blissful embrace, we shall sport today in the boundless Sea of grace; the peal of the sweet bell shall reach and live within me; we shall daily smear ourselves with sacred ashes worn by the Lord; my service shall be the foremost in the midst of the saints; we shall worship the flower-feet which Vishnu Himself knows not. The sweet and red kazhuneer flower shall adorn my crown. My gracious Esan and My Lord should be pleased to visit me in grace.

5. We shall be free from all bonds!

The delusions of maya that are spread out on earth shall cease; we shall bow to the flower-feet that the heavenly ones too do not know; fear of the measureless age shall fly off; hearts of God-mad saints shall rejoice today; the thoughts such as I am male, female, neuter, 'I' and 'We' shall die! We, of unknown name, shall escape the births in plenty. I shall reach the countless mystic power and dwell there. My King and gracious Esan should visit me in grace.

6. Rejoicing in the company of saints!

White ash shall glow on His sacred golden form; adoring hands of great saints shall rain down flowers; the thoughts of slender-waisted maidens shall not be disclosed; the delight from the music of the Lyre shall increase; the feet of the saints shall flourish upon my crown; to save us all, He shall emerge with us; we shall fill every place of the organs with sweet, soothing strains. My Father and ancient master should visit me in grace.

7. State of purity!

The purity and wordless peal of bells shall sound sweet; my inner light shall shoot up and glow forever; the great Supreme shall drive off all diversities. In the ancient Vedas, the salient features of Lord Eswara are specified and through them, countless unusual divine experiences are felt by the pure mind; but when there is no mind in the state of utter purity, there are no such experiences occurring; the wild love from the bow-browed good maidens shall not rise; the Supreme things shall not be unknown to the gods; we shall have the boundless eight-fold excellence. That moon crowned Gem should visit us in grace to save us.

8. Tasting Shiva's Bliss!

The welling blast of sound from the conches shall flourish and we shall get fed up with the caste-bound qualities. The deluded thoughts of this is good and that is good shall cease. All our desires shall be the servants of His own servants. We shall not any longer enjoy the hearts of fish-like, bright-eyed maids. We shall henceforth taste Shiva's bliss which the glorious saints enjoy! We shall also gain the great ambrosial light which is pervasive. The endless Vedin should in grace make us His!

50. Aanandamaalai (The Rapture Garland)

1. Show me the way to join You!

Those who have approached Your bright fair Feet have crossed the mighty world. All the heavenly ones stand worshipping with golden flowers. But I, of mean and stony heart, for which there is no other comparison but me, and rejected by Your own saints, sank in the Sea of griefs. Oh! Speak of how I could henceforth meet You.

2. Here I lie as food for diseases!

You gave me bliss which is unknown! I did not know of it and so lay ruined! You are not to be blamed at all. I have not met Your perfect saints who bow before and praise You always. So, Oh Chief! I have been left behind here as feast for birth-disease. My Lord! who else would save Your slave!

3. He showed me wilderment as well as the way!

I was void of a life of virtues, void of an austere life of love or wisdom and like leather dolls in a puppet whom I whirled and fell and lay prostrate. But He gave me the craze and the ways to reach the world with no exit. He also showed me His form and made me His. Oh! When can I the cruel one meet Him?

4. Is it meet that You do not stand amidst me!

By seeking ruins, I ruined myself and You Oh! the deathless one got the blame. I shall suffer all that is my due, but then, what is the use of suffering! Oh! Gem of a teacher who could prevent my fall in hell and make me Yours, except You, You! Our Lord! wouldn't be just if You should not be just to me?

5. Don't refuse me!

Oh! You who are Mother-like gave me Your Feet! Ah! I called You mother and reached Your Feet and at once You enslaved me that day. Why should You now refuse me that? Won't I, a dog, perish like a weanling calf? Why have you no mercy for me? But why don't You want me now!

6. Shiva is my comfort!

Should You not grace me? Is it just that my cruel self should go to ruin? Oh King! if You would not ask me to come to You, who else would comfort me? Are all the dying ones like me? Would they not say that it is not the way, I am confused! Oh! dancing God at Holy Thillai! comfort me hereafter!

7. I know not what to do!

You converted jackals into steeds and made the whole world know it. You of Perunthurai made all of Tennan's great Madurai city crazy. You are the rare essence! You are the master in Avinashi, You are the flood in Pandiland! Oh! You, the Great splendour, You are too difficult to be known! I do not know anything of what to do!

51. Achchoppathigham (The Hymns of Highest Bliss)

1. He purified my soul and made me Shivam!

I used to move with the brutes who did not know the way to attain Mukthi. He drove off my age-old 'deed' and taught me the path of love. He wiped away my mental bonds and made me His own and made me Shivam. Is it not amazing, for who can thus be blessed with the Father's way of grace?

2. His signless Self disclosed Himself!

I mistook every wrongful way as the righteous way. But He took off the mean ways from me and led me towards sacred grace. There are no signs to know Him the Dancer, but He has well made me know His dance. Is it not amazing, for who can thus be blessed with such a way of grace?

3. He made me reach His Feet alone!

I considered everything that was false to be true and so I was lured by the charms of the maids and went about crazy. But He saved my soul and gave me His grace. The Lord whose Self is Umadevi made me reach His Feet alone. Is it not amazing, for who can be blessed in this way with the Father's way of grace?

4. He adorned me with Holy ash and showed the truthful way!

I would surely fall and die, for I have become tired, being born on this earth. But He gave me love which is beyond all thoughts and He made me His and caused me to wear His white ashes and reach His purest ways. Is it not amazing, for who can in this manner be blessed with the great one's way of grace?

5. He called me and said 'Fear Not'!

I was attacked by the side-glances of the soft-footed maids. I stood with my heart so full of sorrows, but then I got Your grace, also. My Lord! I am saved for You had asked me to come to You and had told me not to fear. Is it not amazing, for who can thus be blessed with Your own way of grace?

6. He rid me of bonds and faints!

I mistook this birth of the body, which is to die, as true and fell upon the breasts of maids and multiplied my sins. But He cut off my ego, my bonds and my flaws and made me His own. Is it not amazing, for who can thus be blessed with gracious salvation?

7. He taught me the meaning of Almighty OM!

I fell and sank within the mania for the maids, but He gently took me and led me, rooting out all my bonds, He taught me the truth of 'OM' and gave me the way of salvation. Is it not amazing, for who can thus be blessed with the Father's way of grace?

8. He saved and graced me!

I faltered and was tossed about in the whirlpool of births and deaths, with lust I sank within the embrace of the maids decked with jewels. The Lord whose half is Umadevi, made me reach His Feet only. Is it not amazing, for who can thus be blessed with the first one's way of grace?

9. He treated me as worthy and placed me in a palanquin!

I was wandering on and on with fools and did not know the Supreme God. But He, the First and Primal Lord, washed away my three-fold dirts. He treated me well and placed my dog-like self which is unworthy on a palanquin! Is it not amazing, for who can thus be blessed with a Mother's way of grace?

10. What is this wisdom which does not know Shivam?

There is the place of births and deaths and the place where there is no death at all. And those who do not know Him and do not know all these things are said to possess no wisdom at all. But He gave me proper land and He gave me everything. He gave me Great Pain too. Is it not amazing, for who can thus be blessed with the Father's way of Grace?

OM SHIVARPPANAM!